The SAGE Guide to Writing in Criminal Justice Research Methods

Sara Miller McCune founded SAGE Publishing in 1965 to support the dissemination of usable knowledge and educate a global community. SAGE publishes more than 1000 journals and over 800 new books each year, spanning a wide range of subject areas. Our growing selection of library products includes archives, data, case studies and video. SAGE remains majority owned by our founder and after her lifetime will become owned by a charitable trust that secures the company's continued independence.

Los Angeles | London | New Delhi | Singapore | Washington DC | Melbourne

The SAGE Guide to Writing in Criminal Justice Research Methods

Jennifer M. Allen
Nova Southeastern University

Steven Hougland
Florida Sheriffs Association

Los Angeles | London | New Delhi
Singapore | Washington DC | Melbourne

FOR INFORMATION:

SAGE Publications, Inc.
2455 Teller Road
Thousand Oaks, California 91320
E-mail: order@sagepub.com

SAGE Publications Ltd.
1 Oliver's Yard
55 City Road
London, EC1Y 1SP
United Kingdom

SAGE Publications India Pvt. Ltd.
B 1/I 1 Mohan Cooperative Industrial Area
Mathura Road, New Delhi 110 044
India

SAGE Publications Asia-Pacific Pte. Ltd.
18 Cross Street #10-10/11/12
China Square Central
Singapore 048423

Printed in the United States of America

Library of Congress Cataloging-in-Publication Data

Names: Allen, Jennifer M., author. | Hougland, Steven M., author.

Title: The Sage guide to writing in criminal justice research methods / Jennifer M. Allen, Nova Southeastern University, Steven Hougland, Florida Sheriffs Association.

Description: First Edition. | Thousand Oaks : SAGE Publications, Inc, 2020. | Includes bibliographical references.

Identifiers: LCCN 2019053679 | ISBN 9781544364711 (paperback) | ISBN 9781544364704 (epub) | ISBN 9781544364698 (epub) | ISBN 9781544364681 (ebook)

Subjects: LCSH: Criminal justice, Administration of—Research—Methodology. | Report writing.

Classification: LCC HV7419.5 .A495 2020 | DDC 808.06/6364—dc23

LC record available at https://lccn.loc.gov/2019053679

This book is printed on acid-free paper.

Acquisitions Editor: Jessica Miller
Editorial Assistant: Rebecca Lee
Production Editor: Bennie Clark Allen
Copy Editor: Lana Todorovic-Arndt
Typesetter: Hurix Digital
Proofreader: Susan Schon
Cover Designer: Candice Harman
Marketing Manager: Kara Kindstrom

20 21 22 23 24 10 9 8 7 6 5 4 3 2 1

Brief Contents

Detailed Contents

Preface

As practitioners in policing and probation, we have seen many reports that did not provide enough information to make a case for court prosecution or treatment and rehabilitation. As educators, we have seen students in criminal justice struggle with researching, writing, citing and referencing, and understanding the processes and procedures of criminal justice without seeing actual reports that mark the progression of a case through the system or the creation of an academic paper. This supplemental text focuses on teaching students how to write about and interpret research methods in the academic setting, while introducing them to a number of other research and writing tools, such as literature reviews, abstracts, proposals, and grant writing. The goal is to interweave professional and applied writing, academic writing, and research methodology, with the result being a stronger, more confident researcher and student in criminal justice.

There are several challenges to conducting and interpreting research in criminal justice: (a) an abundance of previously written literature in many topic areas, (b) the need to locate and interpret credible sources, and (c) understanding how to format and organize literature reviews and proposals. The abundance of literature in any topic area requires students to narrow the topic and focus the research questions so that the literature identified in the topic area is as focused as possible. This will reduce the search results significantly so that students and researchers can more easily identify and evaluate proper sources. Searches can also be limited by using criminal justice databases and search parameters. Next, all source material should be evaluated thoroughly since anyone can post information to the Web. Using an implausible source can discredit an essay and the writer. Finally, the organization of literature reviews and proposals—particularly grant proposals—depends on the research methodology or the grant-providing institution. Students and researchers who organize these assignments improperly risk a poor grade or the loss of grant dollars.

Instructors also sometimes struggle with two issues that are shared by students: (1) writing for fact and (2) brevity. Students and faculty are taught throughout their academic careers to write to page-length requirements. In criminal justice reports, there is no page-length requirement, and the writing process requires the writer to say what needs to be said factually and succinctly. Thus, students have to train themselves to identify the facts and to learn how to write only what is tangible in a report. Instructors have to find a way to teach these skills while introducing critical thinking and information literacy. This can be a challenge for everyone involved.

With these concerns in mind, we have written a concise book that introduces key topics in academic writing and research methods in the criminal justice discipline. We believe that the text is reader-friendly and comprehensive yet concise.

Approach

Universities have historically supported intensive courses in writing and have encouraged writing in the discipline across the various academic fields. However, how this has been accomplished is not always clear and varies tremendously from school to school. Sometimes, writing is taught almost exclusively in English courses, while other times, it includes the efforts of individual criminal justice departments. Regardless of the approach, we believe that criminal justice departments have a responsibility to focus on teaching applied writing to their students because writing is an essential skill in this field. In the process of teaching applied writing, instructors can also prepare students to write well academically by introducing information literacy, critical thinking in writing, and the American Psychological Association (APA) style.

The first chapter of this text focuses on the basics of writing by introducing common grammar errors and the types of writing projects commonly seen in academia and in the field of criminal justice. The second chapter introduces information literacy and digital literacy to students. Chapter 3 provides information on writing literature reviews and abstracts, including examples of each. Research design, methods, and data analysis are described in Chapter 4. Chapter 5 focuses on writing research and grant proposals. Chapter 6 discusses the APA format as well as MLA (Modern Language Association) style and the Chicago style of writing. Finally, Chapter 7 concentrates on the academic research paper by providing students a format to use and information on how to read a scholarly article.

The chapters are enhanced with other features such as

- Chapter summaries

- Narrative and descriptive examples

- Questions for consideration and critical thinking

- *In the News* reports supporting the material discussed

- Applied exercises

Acknowledgments

Even though this is the first edition of this text, we have several individuals to thank for their contributions. We thank the following reviewers of the manuscript for their many helpful suggestions:

Julie Brancale, Western Carolina University

Karen Clark, University of Arizona

Claudia Cox, University of Portsmouth

Joel M. Cox, Liberty University

Dr. Jean Dawson, Franklin Pierce University

Jeffery Dennis, Minnesota State University

Bryn Herrschaft-Eckman, Temple University

Milton C. Hill, Stephen F. Austin State University

Stephen J. Koonz, SUNY Oneonta

Renee D. Lamphere, The University of North Carolina at Pembroke

Anita Lavorgna, University of Southampton

Shana L. Maier, Widener University

Iryna Malendevych, University of Central Florida

Carrie Maloney, East Stroudsburg University

Christina Mancini, Virginia Commonwealth University

Elizabeth B. Perkins, Morehead State University

Selena M. Respass, Miami Dade College

Tiffany J. Samsel, Rowan University

Jeanne Subjack, Southern Utah University

Dr. Mercedes Valadez, California State University, Sacramento

Nick Zingo, California State University, Northridge

About the Authors

Jennifer M. Allen is a full professor at Nova Southeastern University in the School of Criminal Justice. She has worked with juveniles in detention, those on probation, and those victimized by abuse and neglect. Dr. Allen has served on advisory boards for Big Brother/Big Sister mentoring programs, Rainbow Children's Home, domestic violence/sexual assault programs, and teen courts. She has published in the areas of restorative justice, juvenile delinquency and justice, youth programming, police crime, and police administration and ethics. She is also the coauthor of *Criminal Justice Administration: A Service Quality Approach; Juvenile Justice: A Guide to Theory, Policy, and Practice; The Sage Guide to Writing in Criminal Justice; The Sage Guide to Writing in Corrections;* and *The Sage Guide to Writing in Law Enforcement.*

Steven Hougland is a researcher for the Florida Sheriffs Association. Formerly an associate professor of criminal justice, he is a retired law enforcement officer with 30 years of policing and corrections experience at the local and state levels. Dr. Hougland has published in the areas of police use of force, law enforcement accreditation, and police ethics. He is also the coauthor of *The Sage Guide to Writing in Criminal Justice, The Sage Guide to Writing in Corrections* (forthcoming), and *The Sage Guide to Writing in Law Enforcement* (forthcoming).

CHAPTER 1

The Basics of Writing

There is an adage in criminal justice that "if it's not in writing, it didn't happen." This means that criminal justice documents must provide enough details to explain what actually happened at a scene or during an incident or court hearing. Missing details or information that is written vaguely may result in a case being dismissed. Further, a poorly written report could open the door for a mistrial, a not guilty verdict, or the criminal justice worker may appear to have made up the details or to be unsure of the reported details when testifying on the stand. Therefore, it is important that those working in criminal justice understand the complexities of writing quality reports.

Criminal justice officers are required to write many different types of narrative and descriptive documents. In policing and corrections, the basic incident report documents the officer's or inmate's activity; records the actions and testimony of victims, suspects, and witnesses; serves as a legal account of an event; and is used for court testimony or in parole hearings. Being the best writer possible is a necessity for professionals in the criminal justice field.

The need to write well has never been more important. Relating facts about an incident and investigation go far beyond the eyes of the supervisor and agency. A report will convict criminals, encourage the support of the community, and become a guide by which the public and the courts will measure their respect for the criminal justice system and its workers.

Additionally, criminal justice reports are public record in many states. As such, they are available for all to review. Attorneys, paralegals, and staff personnel on both sides of a case, as well as judges and journalists, may read criminal justice reports. Imagine writing a report that is read by a Justice of the Supreme Court!

Similarly, criminal justice professors often require students to complete writing assignments such as essays, case analyses, and legal briefs. These assignments help develop critical thinking skills, as well as research and writing skills required in criminal justice careers.

This chapter introduces students to common writing assignments in the criminal justice and criminology classroom, as well as those required in the criminal justice professions.

Basic Grammar Rules

Studies suggest successful writing skills take much longer to develop. Learning to write an effective, extended text is a vastly complex process that often requires more than two decades of training. A skilled, professional writer progresses beyond writing to tell a story by crafting the narrative with the audience's interpretation of the text in mind (Kellogg, 2008). Paragraphs and sentences form the basis of the text. Writing clear, short sentences is an important element of technical writing.

Any discussion on writing begins with the sentence.

The Sentence

The sentence comprises a subject and a predicate, and the unit must make complete sense. In other words, a sentence must be able to stand alone as a complete thought. Sentences can be one word or a complex combination of words. Criminal justice professionals write all documents using complete sentences, usually in the first person with no slang or jargon. On occasion, corrections documents may be written in the third person, although still with complete sentences that include a subject and a predicate. Sentences should be brief with no structural, grammatical, or spelling errors. The writer must write clear, complete sentences so that the audience can easily understand the writing.

The Subject

The subject is the word that states who or what does the action or is acted upon by the verb. The subject can be expressed or implied. Rephrase the following sentences as questions to identify the subject. So, for number 1, for example, one could ask, "Who reported the crime?" The answer, of course, is the victim, and in this sentence, "victim" functions as the subject.

Examples:

1. The *victim* reported the crime.
   Who reported the crime? The victim.

2. *I* responded to the scene.

3. *I* arrested the defendant.

4. *Deputy Smith* read the defendant his Miranda rights.

5. The *suspect* entered the vehicle through the driver's door.

If a sentence requires a subject and a predicate, can one word function as a complete sentence? Yes, if that word is a command. In a command, the subject is the implied or understood "you."

Examples:

1. "Stop!"
   The subject is not clearly stated, but it is implied or understood to be "you."

2. "Sit down!"

3. "Halt!"

The Verb

The verb is the word or group of words that describes what action is taking place.

Examples:

1. The Deputy *drove*.
   Drove tells what action the subject (Deputy) did.

2. The Deputy *was dispatched* to the call.
   Was dispatched tells what action is taking place.

3. I *arrested* the defendant.

4. *Stop*!
   Remember the subject in a command is the implied "you."

5. I *did not respond* to the call.

Standing Alone and Making Complete Sense

A complete sentence must have a subject and a verb, and it must make complete sense. The sentence must be a complete idea; it must be able to stand alone as a complete thought.

Examples:

Incorrect 1.   The agent.

The subject (agent) lacks a verb and does not make complete sense.

Incorrect 2.   The agent purchased.

The subject (agent) and verb (purchased) lacks complete sense.

Correct 3.   The agent purchased cocaine. (complete sentence)

Incorrect 4.   The agent arrested.

The subject (agent) and verb (arrested) lacks complete sense.

Correct 5.   The agent arrested the defendant. (complete sentence)

Incorrect 6.   The Deputy who responded to the scene. (incomplete sentence)

Correct 7.   The Deputy who responded to the scene arrested the defendant. (complete sentence)

Correct 8.   The agent was working. (complete sentence)

Correct 9.   The agent was working in an undercover capacity. (complete sentence)

Correct 10.   The agent was working in an undercover capacity for the purpose of purchasing cocaine. (complete sentence)

Identify the subject and verb in each of the following examples.

I arrested the defendant.
    I (subject) + arrested (verb).

1. The defendant entered the victim's vehicle.

2. The defendant smashed the driver's door window.

3. He removed a stereo from the dash.

4. The stereo is valued at $300.00.

5. I processed the scene for latent prints.

6. The defendant punched the victim in the face.

7. The suspect removed the victim's bicycle from the garage.

8. I responded to the scene.

9. I arrested the defendant.

10. I transported the defendant to Central Booking for processing.

See answers on p. 22.

Structural Errors

Some of the most common structural errors in criminal justice and academic writing are fragments, run-on sentences, and comma splices. But once identified, they are easily corrected.

Fragments

A fragment is an incomplete sentence.
All of the following are fragments:

1. Entered the vehicle. (no subject)

2. Processed the scene. (no subject)

3. I the scene. (no verb)

4. At the scene. (no subject or verb)

5. I processed. (lacks completeness)

Fragments can be corrected in any one of several ways. After identifying the missing element (subject, verb, or completeness), simply insert the missing element to complete the sentence.

Revised 1.	The defendant entered the vehicle.
Revised 2.	A crime scene technician processed the scene.
Revised 3.	I responded to the scene.
Revised 4.	The defendant was found at the scene.
Revised 5.	I processed the scene.

Run-On Sentences

A run-on sentence is two or more complete sentences improperly joined without punctuation.

Example 1: We arrived at the scene Deputy Smith interviewed the victim.

Sentence 1: We arrived at the scene.

Sentence 2: Deputy Smith interviewed the victim.

Revision Strategy 1. Create two independent sentences.

Revision 1. We arrived at the scene. Deputy Smith interviewed the victim.

Revision Strategy 2. Join the independent clauses with a comma and a coordinating conjunction such as *and, but, for, nor, or, so,* or *yet.*

Revision 2. We arrived at the scene, and Deputy Smith interviewed the victim.

Punctuation Alert! Always place the comma *before* the coordinating conjunction.

Revision Strategy 3. Join the independent clauses with a semicolon if they are closely related ideas.

Revision 3. We arrived at the scene; Deputy Smith interviewed the victim.

Comma Splices

A comma splice is two independent clauses joined improperly with a comma.

Example 1. We arrived at the scene, Deputy Smith interviewed the victim.

Revision Strategy 1. Separate the two sentences by adding a comma followed by a coordinating conjunction before "Deputy Smith."

Revised 1. We arrived at the scene, and Deputy Smith interviewed the victim.

Punctuation

All sentences contain punctuation. Punctuation helps the audience understand the writer's meaning.

> Let's eat Grandma.
> Let's eat, Grandma.
>
> Save a life—use correct punctuation.

Commas

The most frequently used, and misused, punctuation mark is the comma. Use a comma to join two independent clauses with a coordinating conjunction (*and, but, for, or, nor, yet, so*). The comma is always placed *before* the conjunction.

A comma is used to separate a dependent clause from the independent clause.

Example 1:

1. I arrested the defendant, and I booked him into the jail.
    Two independent clauses:
    1. I arrested the defendant.
    2. I booked him into the jail.

A comma is required before the coordinating conjunction.

2. I arrested the defendant and booked him into the jail.
    One independent clause: I arrested the defendant.
    One dependent clause: booked him into the jail. (no subject)

A comma is not used.

More Examples:

1. I interviewed the victim, and she gave a sworn statement.

2. I interviewed the victim, but she refused to give a sworn statement.

A comma is used to separate items in a list. Place a comma before the *and* at the end of the series.

Examples:

1. Deputies Smith, Jones, and White responded to the call. (correct)

2. Deputies Smith, Jones and White responded to the call. (incorrect)

Commas are also used after conjunctive adverbs (however, therefore, and so on). However, if the phrase is very short—less than three words—the comma may be omitted.

Examples:

1. When I responded to the call, I activated my emergency lights and siren.

2. Responding to the call, I activated my emergency lights and siren.

3. Therefore, the findings of my investigation are that no crime took place.

A comma is used to isolate an appositive (a phrase that renames the noun).

Exercise 1.2

Place or remove commas for correct punctuation.

1. We approached the defendant and Deputy Smith asked to buy a "dime."

2. We approached the defendant, and asked to buy a "dime."

3. At today's Day-Shift briefing Sergeant Jones asked for volunteers.

4. I charged the defendant with sale and delivery of cocaine, possession of cocaine and possession of drug paraphernalia.

5. Sergeant Jones the Day-Shift supervisor, asked for volunteers.

6. I arrested the defendant for shoplifting yet he denied the charge.

7. I am usually assigned to Zone 43 but today I am working in Zone 45.

8. Today I wrote reports for burglary, theft and battery.

9. Deputy Smith, an experienced agent made a cocaine seizure today.

See answers on p. 23.

Examples:

1. The man, a white male, was arrested for theft.

2. Deputy Smith, a rookie, was assigned to the midnight shift.

3. My assigned vehicle, car 1042, is a 1991 Ford LTD.

Check if the commas have been placed properly by simply removing the words between the commas. If what remains is a complete sentence, the commas are correctly placed.

Example:

> The man, a white male, was arrested for theft.
>
> Remove the words between the commas: a white male.
>
> What remains, "The man was arrested for theft," is a complete sentence.
>
> The placement of the commas is correct.

The Semicolon

The semicolon indicates a strong relationship between two sentences.

Examples:

1. I interviewed the victim; however, she failed to provide a statement.
2. I arrested the defendant; later, I transported and booked him into the jail.

Exercise 1.3

Insert or remove semicolons for correct punctuation.

1. We responded to the call, Deputy Smith wrote the report.
2. At briefing the sergeant asked for; volunteers and reports.
3. I saw the rescue team treating the victim. She had a stomach wound.
4. The defendant removed the item from the shelf, she then left the store after failing to pay.
5. I am assigned to Sector 4, and I primarily work Zone 43.

See answers on p. 23.

The Colon

The colon is used to introduce a list.

Examples:

1. The defendant was charged with the following: burglary, grand theft, and criminal mischief.

   (Notice the placement of the commas in the series.)

2. Three Deputies responded to the call: Smith, Jones, and Harris.

Insert colons appropriately.

1. I charged the defendant with the following, assault, battery, and theft.

2. The following attachments are provided with this report, sworn statements, tow sheet, and evidence form.

3. I testified on several cases today while in court 92-123456, 90-123456, and 89-123456.

See answers on p. 23.

Quotation Marks

Quotation marks are used to indicate another person's spoken or written words. They are useful in criminal justice documents to indicate statements made by suspects or defendants, responses or comments by victims or witnesses that are particularly relevant to an investigation or anytime an important statement is made. Students also regularly use quotation marks in their academic papers. It is important to remember to only quote from a source when the information cannot be paraphrased in another way, it involves statistics that must be stated exactly, or the point is so important that a student believes it must be stated exactly as the original author wrote. Students should always use quoted material sparingly and attempt to paraphrase or summarize the work as much as possible.

If the quotation is placed at the end of the sentence, a comma is placed before the opening quotation mark. A period is placed within the end quotation mark at the end of the sentence after the in-text citation.

Examples:

1. The defendant stated, "I didn't mean to kill her."

2. I told the defendant, "You're under arrest."

If a sentence begins with a quotation, a comma is placed within the end quotation mark.

3. "I didn't mean to kill her," he said.

If a quotation mark is around a single word or group of words, the punctuation *always* goes inside the quotation mark.

Examples:

1. I asked the suspect if he knew where I could purchase a "dime," the common street reference for $10 of cocaine.

2. The victim told me he had taken LSD and was "high," so I called Rescue for medical treatment.

Exercise 1.5

Punctuate the following sentences properly using quotation marks and commas as needed.

1. The victim said He stabbed me in the stomach.

2. He stabbed me in the stomach she said.

3. I bought three hits of LSD today.

4. Today I bought three hits of LSD two cocaine rocks and a gram of pot.

5. I asked the defendant for a dime and he took me to 1234 18th Street in Zone 42.

6. She said He stabbed me in the stomach; but I saw no wound.

7. The deputy asked, Who called the Police?

8. Who was it who said Live and let live?

See answers on p. 23.

Plurals

Many nouns are changed to the plural form simply by adding an -s or -es to the end of the noun: Officer becomes officers; bus becomes buses. Some nouns, however, form plurals irregularly by changing the spelling of the word. Some of the most common include

man men   woman women   me us I we

Some nouns do not change their spelling at all to form plurals: *deer, sheep, fish, police.*

Some nouns that have a Latin root still use the Latin form of the plural rather than the English -s. Some examples include *datum/data, crisis/crises,* and *memorandum/memoranda.*

Possessives

The possessive form demonstrates a relationship between two nouns.

Examples:

1. The victim's car was burglarized.

2. The defendant's rights were revoked.

3. The vehicle's tires were slashed.

If the noun is plural and ends with an s, add only an apostrophe.

Examples:

1. The victims' cars were burglarized.

2. The defendants' rights were revoked.

3. These are the victims' radios.

4. Here are the officers' guns.

5. The vehicles' tires were slashed.

Capitalization

Capitalize the names of directions when they indicate a specific location, but not when they indicate a general direction.

Examples:

1. South Carolina

2. The defendant fled south on foot.

Capitalize titles only when they precede the person's name.

Examples:

1. Colonel Smith

2. I met with the colonel.

Commonly Misused Words

Homophones are words that look and sound alike but have different meanings. The following are examples of homophones:

Its and *it's*

1. Its shows possession. "You can't judge a book by its cover."

2. It's is the contraction of it is.

There, their, and *they're*

1. There indicates a location. An easy way to remember this is to look for the word "here" within "there." There also functions as an adverb, as in "There are no more calls holding."

2. Their is an adjective. It describes a noun by showing that an object belongs to more than one person or thing: "Their car was burglarized," or "Here is their stolen property," or "The dogs were in their pen."

3. They're is the contraction of they are.

Lie, lay, lain; to recline

1. I will now lie down.

2. Yesterday I lay down.

3. Last week, I had also lain down.

Lay, laid, laid; to place or set down

1. I will now lay my book down.

2. He laid the gun on the ground.

3. He had already laid his gun down.

Exercise 1.6

Insert the correct word.

1. A police patrol car is easily identified by (it's/its) _____ distinctive color scheme.

2. When is shift change? (It's/Its) _____ this weekend.

3. Yes, (there/their/they're) _____ are no bananas.

4. We are going over (there/their/they're) _____.

5. We found (there/their/they're) _____ stolen property.

6. (There/Their/They're) _____ going over (there/their/they're) _____.

7. I will (lie/lay/lain) _____ down now.

8. The suspect (lay/laid) _____ the gun on the ground, and the officer ordered him to (lie, lay, lain) _____ face down.

9. (Who/Whom) _____ responded to the call?

10. Deputy Smith, (who/whom) _____ did you interview at the scene?

11. The people (which/who/that) _____ were arrested during the reverse sting operation were all adults.

See answers on p. 24.

Who and *whom*
   Who is used as a subject; whom is used as an object.

1. Who wrote the report?

2. The Lieutenant asked the Sergeant, "Whom did you have write this report?"

In modern, spoken English, whom is rarely used.

Which, who, and *that*

Use which and that to refer to animals and things. Always use who to refer to people.

1. The horses, which were kept at the stable, jumped the fence to get loose.

2. The Deputies who responded to the call took 2 minutes to arrive.

The Modifier

A modifier is a word or group of words that describes a noun or a verb. Modifiers may appear before or after the word they describe, but the modifier must be logically placed to prevent confusion.

Examples:

1. Correctional Officer Smith's decision to transfer was an *important* career move.

2. The crime scene perimeter was planned *carefully* by the sergeant.

Notice that the modifiers in both sentences can be dropped without changing the meaning of the sentence.

1. Correctional Officer Smith's decision to transfer was a career move.

2. The crime scene perimeter was planned by the sergeant.

Modifiers can easily confuse readers when they are misplaced within a sentence.

Examples:

1. Suffering from a heart attack, Deputy Smith found the victim at her door. (Who had the heart attack?)

Revised

1. Deputy Smith found the victim at her door suffering from a heart attack.

Examples:

Misplaced 1: The female Deputy, while searching the female informant, found the drugs that were sold by Deputy Smith in the woman's pants.

Revised 1: The female Deputy, while searching the female informant, found the drugs in the woman's pants. The drugs were sold by Deputy Smith in the reverse sting operation.

Misplaced 2: Deputy Jones, while on routine patrol, saw the drunk driver who was arrested by Deputy Harris driving south on Kirkman Road.

Revised 2: Deputy Jones, while on routine patrol, saw the drunk driver driving south on Kirkman Road. Deputy Harris arrested the drunk driver.

Spelling

Proper spelling is a vital part of every written document. Just as improper grammar and punctuation is a sign of semi-literacy, so too is improper spelling. A misspelled word screams for the reader's attention and shapes a negative image of the writer. Several misspelled words can have such a negative effect upon the reader that many will simply refuse to continue reading, finding it too difficult to understand the narrative.

Those who write by hand should keep a good dictionary nearby. When writing by computer, do not overly rely on the spell check. While a spell check will identify and correct misspelled words, it will fail to correct homophones. In this sentence, *four* example, the word "for" is misspelled as "four," yet a spell check program would fail to identify the error.

The following is a list of some of the most frequently misspelled words used in criminal justice writing.

accept	attack	disturbance	misdemeanor
accurate	attorney	efficient	paraphernalia
accuse	battery	examination	receive
acquaintance	bruise	fellatio	sergeant
advisable	bureau	felony	sheriff
aggravated	burglary	foreign	subpoena
apparent	canvassed	harass	tattoo
appeal	cemetery	height	trafficking
apprehend	commit	homicide	trespass
apprehension	conceal	interrogate	trying
approximate	confidential	intoxication	unnecessary
argument	conveyance	jewelry	vicinity
armed robbery	counsel	judge	victim
arraignment	criminal	juvenile	warrant
assault	cunnilingus	lieutenant	weight
associate	discipline	marijuana	wounded

Critical Thinking Skills, Academic Writing, and Professional Writing

Being able to identify errors in writing and to write thorough reports and interesting academic papers requires the ability to critically think. A critical thinker will write better because he or she will weed out nonessential information from written documents. Rugerrio (2008) defines critical thinking as "the process by which we test claims and arguments and determine which have merit and which do not" (p. 18). Ennis (2011) adds, "Critical thinking is reasonable, reflective thinking that is focused on deciding what to believe or do" (p. 1). Critical thinking is a foundational goal of the college experience because it is at the core of modern personal, social, and professional life (Paul, 1995). Phillips and Burrell (2009) note critical thinkers overcome biases and false assumptions that impede decision making. As such, critical thinking prepares students for all aspects of life.

Academic writing enhances critical thinking in several key ways. It is a process that requires students to verify the credibility and biases of source material and objectively examine not just their thoughts and beliefs, but also the ideas of those diametrically opposed to their own (Paul, 1995).

Critical thinking is also an essential skill in the criminal justice professions since it is a key piece of problem solving. Common writing assignments in criminal justice classes include a reflective journal, essay paper, research essay, monograph, annotated bibliography, case study, and legal analysis.

Reflective Journal

The reflective journal assignment is designed to capture a student's feelings and responses to an issue. Journals are more than a synopsis or a simple "I think" response to a question. This assignment requires students to thoroughly and critically evaluate a reading assignment by applying current theory, practice, and course materials to assess a problem, issue, or policy.

Essay Paper

A common assignment for students is the essay paper. The narrative and descriptive essay are examples that require no outside research. For these essays, students are asked to tell a story, explain a process, or describe a place or thing. The length of this essay is typically five pages or less, but length can vary according to the course and instructor.

Research Paper

Like the essay paper, the research paper is a commonly assigned project, especially in upper-level courses. Here, students must conduct outside research to identify source materials that either support or refute a thesis. The student must critically analyze sources to ensure the information is from a respected and reliable source and is both current and credible. Although many students feel anxious about writing a research paper, it can be a valuable experience since "many students will continue to do research throughout their career" (Purdue OWL, 2018a).

Monograph

A monograph is an in-depth study of a single subject written by faculty or scholars for an academic audience (Eastern Illinois University, 2016). According to Crossick (2016), the monograph allows for the "full examination of a topic . . . woven together in a reflective narrative that is not possible in a journal article" (p. 15).

Annotated Bibliography

While a bibliography is a list of sources used to research a particular topic or phenomenon, an annotated bibliography provides a summary and evaluation of each source (Purdue OWL, 2018e). The annotated bibliography will include a formatted reference, such as those found in a bibliography, followed by an annotation. Annotations are written in paragraph form and include a summary of the main points of the article, an assessment of how the article relates to the topic, phenomenon, or research question, and a reflection of what may be missing from the article and/or if the source is reliable, biased, and what the goal of the article may be (Purdue OWL, 2018a).

Case Study

A case study is an in-depth analysis of real life events intended to examine individuals, groups, or events in their natural environment (Hancock & Algozzine, 2016). To successfully complete the assignment in criminal justice courses, students are often required to (1) summarize an actual event and identify a problem; (2) provide a detailed explanation of how the problem was addressed or resolved; and (3) critically analyze the resolution by applying course materials, criminal justice theory, and the findings and conclusions of research from previous study of the same or similar problem.

Legal Analysis

The legal analysis assignment is a research paper in which a student must analyze a set of facts within the context of applicable law. Professors often assign a case study as part of a Constitutional Law, State Law, or Civil Law course. Students are required to research judicial opinions, state statutes and constitutions, the United States Constitution, and administrative law (Rowe, 2009). It is particularly important for students to ensure the applied law is not outdated or appealed (Rowe, 2009).

Writing for the Criminal Justice Professions

Thinking critically and writing for academic classes is great practice for the profession of criminal justice. Similarly, the criminal justice professions require a variety of written work. Harvey (2015) notes the most powerful instrument a criminal justice officer carries is a pen. These are strong words considering the many weapons carried by criminal justice practitioners. If a report is poorly written, readers are less likely to take the content seriously and may question the writer's credibility, which, in the criminal justice system, can have serious consequences (Harrison, Weisman, & Zornado, 2017). The following is a short listing of the legal consequences of poorly written reports:

1. Drug case dismissed and inmates released due to bad search warrant (Astolfi, 2016).

2. Killers go free due to incomplete police reports (Haner, Wilson, & O'Donnell, 2002).

3. Police Credibility on Trial in D.C.

   Courts drawing the jury's attention to such a discrepancy—by having an officer read aloud from his arrest report—gives a defense lawyer an opening to explore whether the officer might have been wrong about other important facts (Flaherty & Harriston, 1994).

4. Words Used in Sexual Assault Reports Can Hurt Cases

   Poorly written reports—sometimes laden with implications of disbelief or skepticism— can contaminate a jury's perception of a victim's credibility or cripple a case altogether (Dissell, 2010).

5. Officers Indicted by Federal Grand Jury

   Three Georgia officers charged with writing false reports to cover up police assault (Department of Justice, 2014).

Policing Reports

Police officers are required to write a narrative in many different types of documents. Many agencies use a cover page of check boxes and blank spaces to indicate the type of incident being documented, demographic information, and the address of the parties involved. Many of these same documents, though, require the officer to complete a detailed, written narrative that accurately documents the officer's observations and actions, statements made by victims, witnesses, and suspects, any evidence collected, and other information relevant to the case. Policing documents are often written in a narrative format in which the officer tells a story of his or her involvement in an official event.

The following list represents the most often used documents that require a written narrative.

Field Notes

Field notes are commonly used in policing. Notes taken at a crime scene are vital to the accuracy of initial and follow-up reports. Officers are also able to refer to their field notes to refresh their memory during deposition and trial in most states. Note taking is the process of gathering and recording facts and information relevant to the police investigation. Officers gather a variety of information in a quick and efficient manner so they may recall the facts of the case to write the incident report, assist follow-up investigations, and refresh their memory for court testimony.

Incident Reports

The incident report is the most common type of writing assignment in policing. It is usually written by a patrol officer to officially document a crime reported by a citizen or when the officer makes an arrest. The document serves several purposes. It is a legal document of an officer's actions, observations, and conversations at a crime scene or self-initiated contact with a citizen. Typical reports can range from one to three pages in length, but more serious crimes are often five or more pages. Incident reports are used by investigators, prosecutors, defense attorneys, judges, and the media to evaluate an officer's job performance.

Supplemental Report

This report is an addendum to the incident report. The supplemental report is often used by officers and investigators to add additional information to the incident report. The supplemental report is most often used to document interviews, evidence collected, or other activity related to a case that occurred after an officer's original incident report.

Booking Reports

In addition to an incident report, officers are often required to write a booking report when an arrestee is transported or delivered to a jail. The narrative of a booking report is often just two or three paragraphs since it requires only the details that establish probable cause for the arrest.

Evidence

The evidence report is used to document any item that has been seized by an officer or has evidentiary value. It also establishes a chain of custody so that seized items can be presented in court. Advances in the technology available to criminal justice agencies have expanded the scope of items of evidentiary value to include video and audio recorded on cell phones, body and in-car cameras, housing unit cameras located in adult and juvenile detention facilities, courtroom cameras, and surveillance cameras. This report is also an addendum to the incident report.

Search Warrant

The Fourth Amendment protects against unreasonable searches and seizures, and in general, a search warrant is needed prior to conducting a search.

The search warrant is a written order, signed by a magistrate having jurisdiction over the place to be searched, based upon probable cause, ordering a police officer to search a particular person or place and to seize certain described property. The search warrant must sufficiently describe the place to be searched and the items to be seized very clearly so that any officer executing the warrant would make no mistake locating the property or seizing the proper items.

Grants

Many local criminal justice agencies struggle to continue to offer a level of service enjoyed in the past as revenues shrink and budgets are dramatically reduced. There will always be crime, but criminal justice professionals and professors alike are often forced to find new funding sources to create or test new ideas and programs (Davis, 1999).

Perhaps not often enough, these agencies seek out grant funding to supplement personnel and equipment costs, finance community service programs, and fund new initiatives that otherwise would not be possible. According to Karsh and Fox (2014), a grant "is an award of money that allows you to do very specific things that usually meet very specific guidelines that are spelled out in painstaking detail and to which you must respond very clearly in your grant proposal" (p. 12). The field of criminal justice—academically and professionally—has benefited greatly from grant funding (Davis, 1999).

Grant funds can come from a number of sources including the federal government, corporations, foundations, and even individuals. The federal government, through Grants.gov, is the most prominent grant provider for criminal justice agencies. The United States Department of Justice (DOJ) offers grant funding to local and state law enforcement agencies to "assist victims of crime; to provide training and technical assistance; to conduct research; and to implement programs that improve the criminal, civil, and juvenile justice systems" (DOJ, 2018). Through the Office of Community Oriented Policing, the Office of Justice Systems, and the Office of Violence Against Women, the DOJ provides grants to support the hiring and training of police officers, implementation of crime control programs, and reduction of violence against women (DOJ, 2018). Similarly, the Bureau of Justice Assistance provides grant funding for "law enforcement, prosecution, indigent defense, courts, crime prevention and education, corrections and community corrections, [and] drug treatment" (Office of Justice Programs, 2018). Criminal justice agencies can also establish partnerships with academic institutions. According to Gerardi and Wolff (2008), one such collaborative effort yielded over $6 million to a corrections institution over a 5-year period.

Corrections Reports

Most documents used in corrections do not require a written narrative. Many documents can be effectively completed by selecting a check box or entering demographic or descriptive information in a content box. Like in policing, though, corrections officers often find the need to write an incident report.

Incident Report

Although often written in third person, the incident report narrative written by a corrections officer is very similar to that written by a police officer. This report can be used to officially document most events, including criminal activity, violation of institutional policy, discovered contraband, and incidents between officers and inmates, as well as those between inmates. They may also be used to justify inmate discipline, segregation, or use of force by an officer.

Probation/Parole Reports

Pre-trial Report

A pre-trial report is completed prior to an individual's first appearance in court and recommends whether to release or detain the person before trial (United States Courts, n.d.). This report addresses the defendant's probability of following the law and the court's directives, and it recommends conditions for the court to impose if the defendant is released, such as drug testing or location monitoring (United States Courts, 2018).

Pre-sentence Investigation Report

A pre-sentence investigation and report are completed when a defendant is found guilty at trial or pleads guilty. This report requires an officer to assess an offender's "living conditions, family relationships, community ties, and drug use," among other things (United States Courts, 2018). According to the American Probation and Parole Association (1987), the purpose of the pre-sentence investigation report is to "provide the sentencing court with succinct and precise information upon which to base a rational sentencing decision" (para. 1).

Court Reports

Restraining or Protective Order

A Restraining Order is issued by a court to protect a business or individual from harm. In the case of a business, the order often requires a person not enter buildings and parking lots and to not engage in contact with business employees or customers. Individual orders are most often in the form of a Domestic Violence Injunction. The Domestic Violence Injunction orders an alleged abuser to remain a certain distance away from someone and have no contact with that person.

Victim Impact Statement

The victim impact statement is information from crime victims, in their own words, about how a crime has affected them (National Center for Victims of Crime, 2012). Cassell (2008) notes victims "have this right in all federal sentencings and in virtually all state sentencings" (p. 611). The report offers victims an opportunity to participate in the justice process by describing the physical, psychological, financial, and social harm they have suffered as a result of the crime. It is often provided to the court prior to sentencing an offender and allows a judge to consider information that might otherwise not be available. The victim impact statement is written by a crime victim, but a victim advocate will often assist the victim in writing the document.

Consider the following Victim Impact Statement (Cassell, P. G. [2008]. *In defense of victim impact statements*. Ohio St. J. Crim. L., 6, 618.):

> My name is Susan Antrobus[.] I am the mother of Vanessa Quinn, who was murdered at Trolley Square Mall February 12, 2007. I am writing this letter to you in hopes that you can understand why I feel the need to give an impact statement on behalf of my daughter Vanessa. . . . How has this affected my family[?] [T]o be honest I don't know yet, I can only tell you how it has affected us to this point in time. My Mom gave up her fight for life, 6 weeks after Vanessa was taken from us, and my youngest daughter Susanna had a miscarriage the same night my Mom passed away. My husband and I cry every day, we struggle to get through each and every day, you wake up with it, you carry it through your day and it goes to bed with you every night. All you can do is hope tomorrow will be a little easier [than] today. February 12 has never ended for us; it feels like one long continuous day that will never end. . . . If you're old enough at 18 to give your life up for this country, you're old enough to know what you're doing when you sell an illegal weapon to a minor. I am asking and pleading with this court to give Mr. Hunter the maximum sentence to send a message to the people of this country and people like Mr. Hunter, that if you chose to engage in illegal weapons to minors you will be held responsible for your actions, and maybe some people would get it. . . . It cost us 7,000 dollars to lay our daughter Vanessa to rest. . . . I think I deserve to give an impact statement, since Vanessa is not here to speak for herself, I don't think 10 minutes is asking for much considering what we've lost for a life time. . . .

CHAPTER SUMMARY

Writing well is an important skill for criminal justice students and professionals. Academic writing assignments improve the student's research, critical thinking, and writing skills in preparation for future criminal justice careers. Poor writing can discredit a student, officer, and/or a criminal justice agency's credibility and reputation.

Common writing assignments for criminal justice students include essays, case studies, annotated bibliographies, and legal analysis. In addition to gaining a deeper understanding of criminal justice topics and current issues, assignments such as these enhance critical thinking skills, an essential skill in the criminal justice professions since it is a key piece of problem solving.

Criminal justice professionals are required to write a variety of report narratives, such as an incident report, search warrant, grant, or pre-trial report. As Harrison and colleagues (2017) aptly note, a poorly written report may bring into question the writer's credibility, which, in the criminal justice system, can have serious consequences.

ADDITIONAL READING

Strunk, W. (2011). *The elements of style*. Project Gutenberg. Retrieved from https://www.gutenberg.org/files/37134/37134-h/37134-h.htm

Purdue Online Writing Lab. (2018). General writing resources. Retrieved from https://owl.english.purdue.edu/owl/section/1/

QUESTIONS FOR CONSIDERATION

1. Why is writing well important in criminal justice professions?

2. What functions does the basic incident report serve?

3. Who might read an incident report inside the criminal justice agency? Outside the agency?

4. Define critical thinking. How is critical thinking important to criminal justice students and practitioners?

5. List three documents commonly used in criminal justice agencies. Describe how these documents are used and why they are important.

EXERCISE ANSWERS

Exercise 1.1 Answers

1. defendant (subject) entered (verb).

2. defendant (subject) smashed (verb).

3. He (subject) removed (verb).

4. stereo (subject) is valued (verb).

5. I (subject) processed (verb).

6. defendant (subject) punched (verb).

7. suspect (subject) removed (verb).

8. I (subject) responded (verb).

9. I (subject) arrested (verb).

10. I (subject) transported (verb).

Exercise 1.2 Answers

1. We approached the defendant, and Deputy Smith asked to buy a "dime."

2. We approached the defendant and asked to buy a "dime."

3. At today's Day-Shift briefing, Sgt. Jones asked for volunteers.

4. I charged the defendant with sale and delivery of cocaine, possession of cocaine, and possession of drug paraphernalia.

5. Sgt. Jones, the Day-Shift supervisor, asked for volunteers.

6. I arrested the defendant for shoplifting, yet he denied the charge.

7. I am usually assigned to Zone 43, but today I am working in Zone 45.

8. Today I wrote reports for burglary, theft, and battery.

9. Deputy Smith, an experienced drug agent, made a cocaine seizure today.

Exercise 1.3 Answers

1. We responded to the call; Deputy Smith wrote the report.

2. At briefing the sergeant asked for volunteers and reports.

3. I saw Rescue treating the victim; she had a stomach wound.

4. The defendant removed the item from the shelf; she then left the store after failing to pay.

5. I am assigned to Sector 4; I primarily work Zone 43.

Exercise 1.4 Answers

1. I charged the defendant with the following: assault, battery, and theft.

2. The following attachments are provided with this report: sworn statements, tow sheet, and evidence form.

3. I testified on several cases today while in court: 92-123456, 90-123456, and 89-123456.

Exercise 1.5 Answers

1. The victim said, "He stabbed me in the stomach."

2. "He stabbed me in the stomach," she said.

3. "I bought three hits of LSD today."

4. "Today I bought three hits of LSD, two cocaine rocks, and a gram of pot."

5. "I asked the defendant for a dime, and he took me to 1234 18th Street in Zone 42."

6. She said, "He stabbed me in the stomach"; but I saw no wound.

7. The deputy asked, "Who called the police?"

8. Who was it who said "Live and let live"?

Exercise 1.6 Answers

1. its
2. it's
3. there
4. there
5. their
6. they're, there
7. lie
8. laid, lie
9. who
10. whom
11. who

What Is Information Literacy?

The average person is bombarded with the equivalent of 174 newspapers of data each day (Alleyne, 2011). The Internet, television, and mobile phones have increased the amount of information a person receives by five times as compared to 1986 (Alleyne, 2011). According to researchers at the University of Southern California, the digital age allows people to send out more information by email, Twitter, social networking sites, and text messages than at any other time in history. In 1986, each individual generated approximately two and half pages of information a day; however, in 2007, each person produced the equivalent of six 85-page newspapers daily (Hilbert & Lopez, 2011). Imagine how that may have changed in the last decade! As one can guess, all of this information has to be stored and catalogued. It also has to be analyzed and sorted using our own interpretations and those presented by the media and other outlets. In a world where fake news and social media dominate most of what people read and hear each day, individuals have to be more savvy and use more critical thinking than ever in distinguishing good information from bad information. Individuals also have to be skilled in acquiring facts and in deciding when information is needed and what to take from the data they gather. In other words, people have to be competent in *information literacy*. In this chapter, information literacy will be defined, and the skills needed to become an information literate person will be identified. Additionally, information literacy and its relationship to technology and critical thinking will be discussed. Examples of how information literacy is used in criminal justice will be provided throughout the chapter.

Information Literacy

Information literacy is not just another buzzword. It is a skill that people can develop over time with the proper understanding of research, analysis, and writing. Information literacy is a crucial talent in the pursuit of knowledge, and it is required in the professional world. It is important in workforces that require lifelong learning, like criminal justice, and it is seen as a linking pin to economic development in education, business, and government (National Forum on Information Literacy, 2018). The National Forum on Information Literacy (2018, para. 3), sponsored by the American Library Association, defined information literacy as a person's ability to "know when they need information, to identify information that can help them address the issue or problem at hand, and to locate, evaluate, and use that information effectively." Most colleges and universities recognize that students should be informationally literate when they graduate. In fact, in 2000, the Association of Colleges and Research Libraries developed the Information Literacy Competency Standards for Higher Education, and in 2004, the American Association for Higher Education and the Council of Independent Colleges endorsed the standards (Stanford's Key to Information Literacy, 2018). Information literacy is considered a key objective for many university and discipline-specific accrediting bodies. Supporting this goal is the belief that information literacy is linked to critical thinking (another objective commanded by colleges and accrediting agencies) because the two skills appear to share very common objectives (Breivik, 2005).

Like information literacy, critical thinking skills require individuals to explore and evaluate ideas for the purpose of forming opinions, problem-solving, and making decisions (Wertz et al., 2013). It has been argued that in both critical thinking and information literacy, individuals must collect information and evaluate its quality and relevance. Then, the individuals must integrate the information into their current understandings or belief systems on particular topics. Finally, in both critical thinking and information literacy, individuals must use the information to draw conclusions and understand the limitations of the information on those conclusions (Wertz et al., 2013). According to Wertz et al. (2013), doing all of this allows for effective decision making.

Other researchers, like Breivik (2005), have argued that it requires critical thinking skills to be information literate because individuals need to analytically assess the information overload they encounter when using technology. Further, a study of digital classrooms in Hong Kong (Kong, 2014) found that using digital classrooms to enhance domain knowledge also increased critical thinking skills among secondary students in a 13-week trial period. However, not all researchers are convinced there is a direct correlation between information literacy and critical thinking. Ward (2006) argued that information literacy goes beyond critical thinking by forcing individuals to manage information in creative and meaningful ways, not to just analyze it. Albitz (2007) claimed that information literacy is skill based, while critical thinking requires higher order cognitive processes. Finally, Weiler (2005) stated that students in the early years of college may be able to find and access information but may not yet have the ability to critically analyze it because they have not developed beyond a dualistic intellectual capacity. Thus, even though a student may find the information needed, they may wait for an authority figure, like a professor, to tell them the answer to the problem. The actual relationship between information literacy and critical thinking skills may well be a chicken-and-egg argument wherein the question is if a person needs critical thinking skills to develop information literacy or if information literacy can increase critical thinking skills. It is likely that the two are intertwined. Regardless of the answer to this question, there appears to be enough evidence to convince universities and accrediting bodies that both skills are absolutely required to produce effective, productive, and successful students and employees.

Just like students are expected to use critical thinking in their academic work, information literacy is common today in all academic disciplines and is used in all learning environments. Many times, students are exposed to

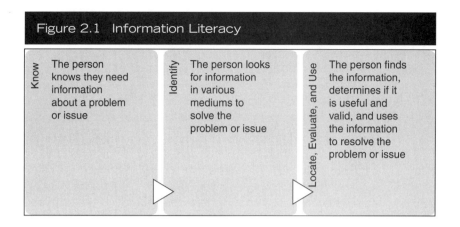

Figure 2.1 Information Literacy

Know — The person knows they need information about a problem or issue

Identify — The person looks for information in various mediums to solve the problem or issue

Locate, Evaluate, and Use — The person finds the information, determines if it is useful and valid, and uses the information to resolve the problem or issue

activities in classrooms that are designed to build skills in information literacy without even realizing it. Most students in college have probably used information literacy to write a research paper or to respond to a class assignment. But gathering information on a single topic does not just stop there. The information has to be analyzed for usefulness and presented in a way that solves a problem or provides more focus to an issue. Information literacy requires that a person also uses the information gathered in ethical and legal ways and that he or she assumes greater control over the investigation and becomes more self-directed in the pursuit of knowledge (Association of College and Research Libraries, 2000). In fact, the Information Literacy Competency Standards for Higher Education require that an information literate person

1. Determine the extent of information needed

2. Access the needed information effectively and efficiently

3. Evaluate information and its sources critically

4. Incorporate selected information into one's knowledge base

5. Use information effectively to accomplish a specific purpose

6. Understand the economic, legal, and social issues surrounding the use of information, and access and use information ethically and legally (Association of College and Research Libraries, 2000, pp. 2–3)

Information literacy is related to information technology skills and extends beyond reading a book or listening to the news. Information literacy includes the technology-enriched digital information world. People use *digital literacy skills* when they rely on technology to communicate with family and friends; *computer literacy skills* when they use hardware, software, peripherals, and network components; and *technology literacy* to work independently and with others to effectively use electronic tools to access, manage, integrate, evaluate, create, and communicate information (Stanford's Key to Information Literacy, 2018). Each of these skills is interwoven with and overlaps the broader concept of information literacy, as information literate individuals will inevitably develop skills in technology during their pursuit of information.

Using Information Literacy—Know, Identify, Evaluate, and Use

As suggested by the Information Literacy Competency Standards for Higher Education (Association of College and Research Libraries, 2000), information literate individuals will follow a process in identifying and using information to resolve problems or issues. This process requires the person to know, identify, evaluate, and use information effectively, ethically, and legally. This process is summarized in the paragraphs that follow.

Know of a Problem or Issue That Needs to Be Resolved

A person may become aware of a problem or issue in a variety of ways. The person may experience a situation that bothers him or her and makes the individual want to resolve it so no one else experiences the same situation. Consider the case of Megan Kanka, who was kidnapped, sexually assaulted, and murdered by a man who had two previous convictions for sexual offenses. He moved into a home directly across the street from Megan prior to the crime. Neither Megan's parents nor their neighbors knew of his background. After her murder and the efforts of her parents to prevent similar crimes in other areas, Megan's Law was passed. Megan's Law created a sex offender notification system, which provides information on sex offenders to communities when a potentially dangerous sex offender moves into the neighborhood (Larson, 2016). Every state now tracks sex offenders and provides information to the public on them.

A person may be told that there is a problem or issue—perhaps through a meeting (e.g., inmates are complaining about an increased number of bugs in the cells), by constituents (e.g., a citizen writes a letter to the mayor complaining that inmates are cleaning the community center while children are present), on the news or through social media (e.g., a friend posts a video on Facebook of a correctional officer abusing an inmate), or by noticing a pattern in data (e.g., court statistics show increases in minority incarceration rates). A student, for example, may be told to complete an assignment by a teacher that seeks to solve a problem or make recommendations about a social issue, like child abuse. Knowing about the problem or issue allows for the process of information literacy to start.

Identify Information

Once a person is aware that there is a problem or issue that he or she needs to resolve, the individual will begin the information gathering process. There are a couple of avenues a person may choose to gather information. He or she may use an information retrieval system, like the library or a database. A probation response, for example, may identify a high number of homeless offenders by using case data on parolees. Another option is for a person to use lab-based activities or simulations to gather information.

For example, to identify weaknesses in the institution's perimeter, a correctional facility may hold mock emergency scenarios that replicate riots or a prison escapes. A third approach may be for the person to use an investigative technique, like surveys or interviews. For example, a corrections officer may discuss concerns about food, safety, or housing with inmates. Once the officer learns that inmates feel unsafe because of increased gang activity or overcrowding, the officer can decide what to do with the remarks. Physical examination can also be used to gather information. Viewing and photographing a crime scene firsthand or witnessing an event with your own eyes can provide a wealth of information about an issue or problem. As an example, an imate may report on increased officer harassment during the evening shift at the prison. Rather than taking the inmate's word, a warden may have shift supervisors watch security cameras for officer activity and/or work in each unit during the shift, so they can witness the officer-inmate interactions for themselves. Witnessing the interactions provides the information needed for the warden to evaluate and determine the best course of action for the criminal activity.

Evaluate the Information

The person who is adept at information literacy will find the information he or she is looking for using various mediums, as discussed above. Then, the person will evaluate the abundant pieces of information found. In the evaluation process, the person is tasked with trying to determine whether the information is valid and reliable. The sources of the information should be examined critically to determine if the source is credible. To do this, the Centers for Disease Control and Prevention (n.d.) suggests that the information literate person assess the information by asking several questions:

1. **Where did the information come from?** This consideration is focused exclusively on the source of the information. In the case of information retrieval systems, the person may assess the journal article and the journal in which the article was published. The information literate person may read the introduction of the journal to determine if the journal is scientific and if the article was peer reviewed. Knowing that an article that undergoes peer review is much more reliable than an article published in a magazine allows the information literate person to accept the information in the article as trustworthy. Using an example from above, the probation officer who evaluates parolee case data and who is familiar with the validity and reliability of these data can make a logical and well-informed decision about how best to handle the increasing number of homeless parolees.

2. **How does the new information fit with what is already known about the problem or issue?** The corrections officer who discussed issues and concerns with inmates may want to compare these complaints with menus in the cafeteria, inmate daily population statistics as related to housing, and inmate characteristics and affiliations. He may also want to talk to other

corrections officers who work with inmates to see if they are noticing increasing conflicts among inmates or issues with space and meals. Comparing the various pieces of information to one another and to information that was gathered previously allows the individual to determine which pieces of data to keep and which to discard. If the officer has worked as a corrections officer for a while, he may already know where the issue lies.

3. **Is funding involved in the creation of the information?** Although funding may not be a part of every equation in solving an issue or problem, the ability to report findings in a study without bias can be skewed if the researcher writing the report has been funded by an outside source. In other words, the source of the funding for a research project may bias the reporting of the results. If funding is present, the source (e.g., journal article, news report) should include that information. When reading an article or listening to a report, the information literate person needs to consider if the funders had anything to gain by the results. If so, questions of validity and credibility in the findings may exist. Consider the findings of a study on a youth mentoring program where the employees of the program completed the data analysis and where the study was paid for using program funds. If the study results demonstrated that the program was not working, the program may be closed, and the employees would need to find another job. If the funders did not have a stake in the results of the study, the funding will likely have less influenced the findings. A person evaluating the information for legitimacy should always contemplate the existence of funding.

4. **Can you trust the information from television, magazines, the Internet, and brochures?** Some reports in the media are based on peer-reviewed journal articles but some are not. Again, when hearing a report, one has to question where the information came from—the source—not who is reporting the information. Accordingly, a person should not just believe ABC News when they report record numbers in parole violations; instead, the individual should listen for the source of ABC News' information, which is hopefully the Federal Bureau of Prisons. The information literate person should also question if the information is consistent with previous information. For example, the media may claim that a finding is conclusive even though a single study's findings are never considered irrefutable, and other media outlets may be providing information in contrary to the news story. The information literate person must recognize that news stories focus on what is "new" and "exciting." Television stations need to sell advertising space to stay in business, and advertisers want to buy advertising space on television stations with the most number of viewers. The same goes for magazines and businesses that produce brochures. Funding may play a key role in the types of stories reported and/or the focus of the stories.

You are a probation officer. You receive a call about a probationer being involved in a domestic disturbance at a home on the south side of town. As you arrive at the home, you see two adults and four children standing in the yard. There are also three neighbors standing in the street. You know that you must use information literacy skills to determine what to do in the current situation. Using each of the skills identified in the chapter—know there is a problem, locate information, evaluate information, use and share the information—explain what steps you will take to resolve the domestic issue and the probation violation that may have occurred.

Thanks to President Trump, few people are not aware of the term *fake news*. Fake news seems to be all the buzz these days. Although it may not be a new trend, it has historically been used in news satire, the fact that the information shared in fake news is widely accepted as a reality is concerning. Fake news articles exist on television, in magazines, and most popularly, on social media and the Internet. Fake news can include completely made-up stories that resemble credible journalism; stories that are only a little bit fake, such as stories that report actual truth but use distorted or decontextualized headlines to convince people to click on their web links; and news stories that are satirical or sarcastic (Hunt, 2016). Oftentimes, the goal behind fake news on the Internet is to entice a reader to click on the story and visit a website to gain advertising revenue for the person hosting the website. According to a report in the *Guardian*, a man who was running a fake news website in Los Angeles told National Public Radio that he has made as much as $30,000 a month from advertising that rewards high traffic to his website (Hunt, 2016). Identifying fake news can be rather difficult, especially in criminal justice; however, the In the News 2.1 shows an example of fake news involving political fraud. The story was published on the Internet and spread through social media, reaching over 6.1 million people before it was discredited by Snopes.com (Garcia & Lear, 2016).

Spotting fake news and evaluating it is not easy because society is flooded with news stories all day, every day. Taking the time to assess and evaluate each one may be an impossibility. However, the information literate individual can rely on the skills he or she has learned to evaluate information to spot fake news. He or she can also look for fake news indicators, such as websites with red flags in their names like ".com.co" and by looking at a website's "About Us" page to determine the website's sources. The individual can use Google Chrome plugins to filter fake news articles from their Internet searches and can google the sources of any quotes or figures in articles he or she may read on the Internet or on social media. Additionally, the information literate person should question websites that he or she has never heard of before. Obscure websites or websites that end in ".org" may have an agenda behind their reporting practices (Hunt, 2016). Finally, using websites to fact check an article, like Snopes.com, which is a fact-checking website with more than 20 years of information, may help to evaluate the credibility of the information provided.

The authors of this book would be remiss if we did not mention that students should be cautious when using the Internet for research and information

Thousands of Fake Ballot Slips Found Marked for Hillary Clinton http://yournewswire.com/thousands-ballot-slips-hillary-clinton/

October 1, 2016, by Baxter Dmitry

Reports are emerging that "tens of thousands" of fraudulent ballot slips have been found in a downtown Columbus, Ohio, warehouse, and the votes are all pre-marked for Hillary Clinton and other Democratic Party candidates.

Randall Prince, a Columbus-area electrical worker, was performing routine checks of his company's wiring and electrical systems when he stumbled across approximately one dozen black, sealed ballot boxes filled with thousands of Franklin County votes for

OFFICIAL GENERAL ELECTION BALLOT

COLS 1+E 01

| A | | Franklin County, Ohio | B | | General Election | C | | November 8, 2016 |

Instructions to Voter

• **To vote:** completely darken the oval (●) to the left of your choice.

• Note the permitted number of choices directly below the title of each candidate office. Do not mark the ballot for more choices than allowed. Vote either "Yes" or "No," or "For" or "Against," on any issue.

• If you mark the ballot for more choices than permitted, that contest or question will not be counted.

• **To vote for a write-in candidate:** completely darken the oval (●) to the left of the blank line and write in the candidate's name. Only votes cast for candidates who filed as write-in candidates can be counted.

• Do not write in a candidate's name if that person's name is already printed on the ballot for that same contest.

• **If you make a mistake or want to change your vote:** return your ballot to an election official and get a new ballot. You may ask for a new ballot up to two times.

For President and Vice President (Vote for not more than 1 pair)	For U.S. Senator (Vote for not more than 1)	For Prosecuting Attorney (Vote for not more than 1)
A vote for any candidates for President and Vice President shall be a vote for the electors of those candidates whose names have been certified to the Secretary of State.	○ Scott Rupert — Nonparty Candidate	○ Bob Fitrakis — Green
	● Ted Strickland — Democratic	● Zach Klein — Democratic
○ For President **Jill Stein** For Vice President **Ajamu Baraka** Green	○ Tom Connors — Nonparty Candidate	○ Ron O'Brien — Republican
	○ Joseph R. DeMare — Green	**For Clerk of the Court of Common Pleas** (Vote for not more than 1)
○ For President **Donald J. Trump** For Vice President **Michael R. Pence** Republican	○ Rob Portman — Republican	● Maryellen O'Shaughnessy — Democratic
	○	○ Besa Sharrah — Republican
	Write-In	**For Sheriff** (Vote for not more than 1)
● For President **Hillary Clinton** For Vice President **Tim Kaine** Democratic	**For Representative to Congress (15th District)** (Vote for not more than 1)	● Dallas L. Baldwin — Democratic
	● Scott Wharton — Democratic	**For County Recorder** (Vote for not more than 1)
	○ Steve Stivers — Republican	○ Daphne Hawk — Republican
○ For President **Richard Duncan** For Vice President **Ricky Johnson** Nonparty Candidates	**For State Representative (18th District)** (Vote for not more than 1)	● Danny O'Connor — Democratic
		For County Treasurer (Vote for not more than 1)
	○ Kristin Boggs	○ Ted A. Berry — Republican

Hillary Clinton and other Democratic Party candidates.

"No one really goes in this building. It's mainly used for short-term storage by a commercial plumber," Prince said.

So when Prince, a Trump supporter, saw several black boxes in an otherwise empty room, he went to investigate. What he found could be evidence of an alleged election fraud operation designed to deliver Clinton the crucial swing state.

Early voting does not begin in Ohio until October 12, so no votes have officially been cast in the Buckeye state. However, inside these boxes were, what one source described as, "potentially tens of thousands of votes" for Hillary Clinton.

An affiliate in Ohio passed along a replica of the documents found in the boxes:

It is important to note that the above replica coincides with a ballot that a Franklin County voter would cast at the polling place on Election Day, meaning the Clinton campaign's likely goal was to slip the fake ballot boxes in with the real ballot boxes when they went to official election judges on November 8th.

Ohio, a perennial swing state in the presidential election, has been a challenge for Clinton and her Democrat counterparts in 2016. Many national Democrat groups have pulled funding from the state entirely, in order to redirect it to places in which they are doing better.

Clinton herself has spent less time in Ohio, and spent less money, in recent weeks as it has appeared that Trump will carry the crucial state.

With this find, however, it now appears that Clinton and the Democrat Party planned on stealing the state on Election Day, making any campaigning there now a waste of time.

This story is still developing, and more news will be published when we have it.

Source: "Thousands of Fake Ballot Slips Found Marked for Hillary Clinton," Baxter Dmitry, YourNewsWire.com. October 1, 2016.

gathering in the first place. Libraries, both electronic and brick-and-mortar, are still the best and most consistent places to find legitimate information. Even though the Internet provides a plethora of information, not all of it is reliable. Anyone can publish anything they want (as long as it is not illegal) on the Internet, even going so far as to make the website where the information published looks genuine. Unlike journal articles that may undergo peer review, websites are not monitored for quality, accuracy, or bias. A popular example of this is Wikipedia.org. Students often refer to and cite Wikipedia in research papers, and Wikipedia claims to be an encyclopedia. Yet Wikipedia is an information website with "openly editable content" (Wikipedia: About, 2018, para. 1). Anyone with access to the Internet can modify a page on the Wikipedia.com website, and anonymous contributors edit most of the content on the website. Although Wikipedia.org contends that the information contributed must be verifiable and come from a reliable source, anyone can post information on Wikipedia.org about a topic whether he or she knows anything about the topic or not (Wikipedia: About, 2018, para. 4). Thus, it is especially important that the information literate person evaluate or use critical thinking skills to assess the resource closely on Wikipedia and all other websites.

When evaluating websites, individuals should consider whether the name of the author or creator of the information is published on the website. He or she should also consider the author or creator's credentials. Asking questions about the author or creator's occupation and experience with the subject matter, position, or education is crucial. Additionally, the information literate person should determine if the author is qualified to write about the topic and if there is contact information for the author or creator somewhere on the website. Another factor to consider is if the author or creator is writing for or associated with an organization. In other words, could their role in the organization potentially influence what is published on the website? The reader may also want to take into account the URL identification and domain name. Domain names with ".org" indicate an affiliation with an organization, while ".com" and ".biz" may be commercial or for-profit websites. Domain names like ".edu" and ".gov" commonly publish articles that have undergone review and may be scientific in nature, although it is still the reader's responsibility to determine their legitimacy by considering the other features of the website.

Although using a search engine, like Google, Yahoo, Bing, or Ask, is a simple way to find websites and articles on a topic, the information literate person has to comb through the web links provided using the factors discussed above to identify those that are most beneficial and valid. Aside from the random Internet websites that may appear in a web search, there are collections of works on search engines, like Google Scholar, where the information literate person can identify scholarly articles from a number of disciplines. Most of the articles on Google Scholar are peer reviewed and provide the author's name, citation, and location where the article is published. Google Scholar regularly provides links to libraries or websites on the Internet where students can find additional scholarly articles on the topic. Regardless of the type of Internet resource an information literate person chooses to use, asking questions about the purpose, objectivity, accuracy, reliability, credibility, and currency of each website is key to identifying appropriate information (Georgetown University Library, 2018).

Finally, it is during the evaluation process that information is deemed relevant, not relevant, or invalid. This is where critical thinking skills are most important, as the individual analyzes and assesses each piece of information. Relevant information is kept for future use while the information literate person dismisses information considered not relevant or invalid. The person then moves into the final phase of the process—*using the information effectively, ethically, and legally.*

Use the Information Effectively, Ethically, and Legally

Once the information literate person identifies the new information, he or she will consider it in combination with prior information and use all of the information to effectively resolve a problem or issue. In using the information, the individual will organize the information and present it in a way that provides a resolution to the problem or issue. The information literate person may write a paper or proposal or do a presentation to an interested audience. The information literate person may also create or implement policy or use the information for their personal lifestyle or work changes. In whatever way the individual uses the information, he or she should strive to share it with an audience through technology or personal communication.

The information acquired should also be used ethically and legally. This requires the information literate person to understand the ethical, legal, and socioeconomic issues involved with the information and the medium in which it is shared. Issues such as privacy and security in printing, posting, or broadcasting should be considered. The individual should also consider censorship and freedom of speech issues as well as copyright and fair use laws (Association of College and Research Libraries, 2000).

Copyright laws protect original works of authorship to include literary, dramatic, musical, and artistic works, as well as computer software and architecture. Copyright laws do not protect ideas, facts, systems, or methods of operations; however, the way these are extracted may be protected (U.S. Copyright Office, n.d.). To ethically use information and under copyright laws, individuals are required to provide credit to the original authors of works when using a protected work. If they do not and the originator finds out, he or she can sue the person who used the work without credit or permission. Fair use laws are a clause in the copyright laws that allow non-profit and educational institutions and libraries to reproduce works from original authors, prepare derivative works from the original works, and distribute copies of original works by sale or lease or other means. These entities can also perform the work publicly to include digital audio transmission and to display the copyrighted work (U.S. Copyright Office, n.d.). Although specific guidelines are attached to fair use, like the inability to photocopy textbooks or distribute copyrighted information to others, providing commentary, criticism, news reporting, and using copyrighted material in research and scholarship are allowable (when credit is provided to the original author). Individuals can also ethically and legally use information in the public domain. Although many believe that all of the information found on the Internet is public domain, this is not true. Works that fall within the public domain include those in which the intellectual property rights have expired, been forfeited, been waived, or where they do not apply. U.S. government documents are excluded from copyright law and are considered as public domain. All other works, even those found on the Internet, are the intellectual property of the person who created them and fall within copyright-protected statutes. Information literate individuals must be diligent in their understanding of how information falls within copyright, fair use, and public domain regulations. These parameters are country based and can vary—meaning what is copyrighted in one country may be public domain in another (U.S. Copyright Office, n.d.). As such, providing credit to the originator or gaining permission to use the work is always the safest approach. The Digital Copyright Slider (2012) created by Michael Brewer and the American Library Association Office for Information Technology Policy is a practical guide for determining copyright, fair use, and public domain.

Developing information literacy skills takes time and effort. Information literate individuals practice the skills by becoming better and more efficient at locating, analyzing, and using the information. Often this practice requires the person to use technology in the process. Thus, he or she develops digital literacy, computer literacy, and technology literacy skills in addition to information literacy skills.

Digital Literacy, Computer Literacy, and Technology Literacy Skills

The information literate person will develop digital, computer, and technology literacy skills as he or she investigates topics using information literacy. These skills will likely become more effective over time and will greatly assist in gathering and dispersing information. Developing these skills allows collaboration with individuals near and far and dissemination of information beyond the intended audiences. As such, these skills, like being information literate, should be used within ethical and legal guidelines, namely privacy, copyright, confidentiality, and authorship.

Digital literacy is the "ability to use information and communication technologies to find, evaluate, create, and communicate information, requiring both cognitive and technical skills" (American Library Association, 2018, para. 2). Digital literacy includes reading digital content and using digital formats to find and create content. For example, reading a book on a Kindle is digital literacy, as is using a search engine to find an article on a sex offender treatment program and sharing the results of a therapy session video with friends and family on social media. Another example is sending an email or tweeting about a weekend activity.

Digital literacy includes digital writing, which may involve emailing, blogging, tweeting, and so on. Digital writing is intended to be shared with others, so understanding its role in the social, legal, and economic community is important. Digital writing can be a potentially precarious tool if the information literate person does not consider the privacy implications of what he or she creates and shares and/or the safety and legal implications of sharing the information (Heitin, 2016). Consider an example where a 13-year-old girl takes a picture of her genitals and Snapchats it to a boyfriend. If the boyfriend saves the photo and sends it to other friends, he may face criminal charges for distributing child pornography. By receiving the picture, he may also face criminal charges if he fails to report the photo to the proper adult or authority. The girl may face criminal charges for distributing child pornography. In this scenario, the picture may travel phone-to-phone through many youth, each facing their own privacy and legal issues when they receive, open, view, and, possibly, share the photo. The moral here is there is an increased responsibility that comes with digital writing and literacy that may not be as pressing in print writing. Print writing, depending on the source, customarily undergoes review before being disseminated, whereas digital information may not.

Computer literacy means that an individual has the basic knowledge and skills to use a computer. The person may be familiar with turning the computer on and off, word processing, printing documents, and so on. As the individual uses the computer, he or she may become even more literate in using other types of programs, operating systems, software applications, and web design. Computer literacy

> can be understood in the same way that traditional literacy applies to print media. However, because computers are much more advanced than print media in terms of access, operation and overall use, computer literacy includes many more types of cognitive and technical skills, from understanding text and visual symbols, to turning devices on and off or accessing parts of an operating system through menus. (technopedia.com, 2018, para. 2)

Being able to code, develop web pages, and network administration are higher level skills developed by some computer literate individuals.

Although not everyone will develop computer literacy skills comparable to a technical support assistant, most information literate individuals develop enough skills to surf the web, identify sources, develop documents and presentations, and disseminate information through the appropriate computer venues. For example, a corrections officer presenting training on prison paraphernalia may develop a PowerPoint presentation. A web technician employed by a state department of corrections to maintain the department's website may post updated incarceration statistics, mission statements, and pictures of corrections officers working in the prison.

Exercise 2.2

What ethical issues might an individual who posts information on social media encounter? What about legal issues? Provide an example post and discuss both the ethical and legal issues.

There are individuals who develop computer literacy skills but use them for illegal activity. They may create viruses, hack websites, and send out bogus or scam emails. The AARP reported in a survey of more than 11,000 Internet users that two-thirds received spam emails at least once per year (Paulas, 2016). Less computer literate individuals may fall prey to these phishing emails, especially if the emails closely mimic bank websites or formal notices from other businesses. Although the police and other social service agencies provide notices when illegal computer activity is flourishing in a specific geographical location, they cannot protect everyone from unethical computer practices. Classes designed to train people in computer literacy can be used to lower the potential for computer victimization, but these often require having discretionary money to pay for the classes. This is something some individuals may not find affordable. The information and computer literate individual will learn over time how to identify and avoid harmful computer practices and will observe legal standards when using the computer.

Quite simply, technology literacy is the ability to use the appropriate technology to communicate and search for information. In technology literacy, a person knows when to use the Internet versus email or when to create a webpage versus a PowerPoint presentation. A prison population analyst, for example, would know when to use an Excel spreadsheet to disseminate inmate population statistics instead of using SPSS, a statistical analysis software package. Developing technology literacy skills is an ongoing process, as instructional and communications technologies change with every new invention. Computers and email are just the tip of the iceberg, as there now exist digitized kitchen appliances, self-driving vehicles, and integrated manufacturing. Who knows what the future holds with regard to technology? Regardless, most agree that technology literacy incorporates four basic skills: (1) the ability to adapt to rapid and continuous technology change; (2) the ability to develop creative solutions to technological problems; (3) the ability to process technological knowledge effectively, efficiently, and ethically;

and (4) the ability to assess technology's place in social, cultural, economic, and legal environments (Wonacott, 2001). Developing and using these skills in conjunction with information literacy is vital to identifying information and using it to solve problems. It is also essential to workplace productivity, decision making, global integration, and, on a more micro level, to finding and keeping a job.

In summary, the information literate person who develops digital, computer, and technology literacy is more likely to continue learning, and developing new and better critical thinking skills. Additionally, they are likely to display other skills desired in the workplace, such as evaluation, analytical thinking, creativity, problem-solving, and research analysis and design skills. The literate person will demonstrate effective skills in decision making, such as acting in moral and ethical ways, and exercise more autonomy and positive work habits (Wonacott, 2001). Each of these skills is essential in the field of criminal justice.

CHAPTER SUMMARY

Information literacy is an acquired skill that allows individuals to know that they need information and to locate, evaluate, use, and share information. Information literacy is usually used to solve problems. Information literate individuals may use a variety of methods to find information, including media, print, the Internet, and other forms of technology. When doing so, the information literate individual is also developing skills in digital, computer, and technology literacy. All forms of literacy discussed in this chapter should be used within ethical and legal considerations. Knowing how the information a person disseminates can affect the social, cultural, economic, and legal environments is especially important in a global society.

Information literate individuals have better chances to acquire and keep jobs. They are more likely to display the types of skills employers demand to include critical thinking, evaluation, creativity, higher morals and ethics, and problem-solving abilities, among others. Workplace productivity can be greatly improved when organizations hire information literate persons. In criminal justice, being able to acquire, evaluate, use, and share information is an essential skill applied in every position and in all cases and interactions. When criminal justice professionals are not adept at information literacy, they can ruin cases, cause appeals, and, in general, prevent the system from functioning effectively.

QUESTIONS FOR CONSIDERATION

1. How might a police officer use technology literacy to do his or her job?

2. Your college professor assigns you a paper for a class project. Using information, digital, computer, and technology literacy, explain how you would complete the project.

3. What confidentiality issues would a parole officer face in gathering and sharing information about parolees?

CHAPTER 3

Writing Literature Reviews and Abstracts

S cholarly articles and essays written for the graduate-level criminal justice course often require writing abstracts and literature reviews. Professors who teach undergraduate courses may require a literature review as well. The literature review is a summary of what the literature says about a specific topic (Purdue Online Writing Lab [OWL], 2018d). It is not an annotated bibliography that links together several abstracts. Rather, the review is written in a narrative style using sources to support the author's ideas on a research topic, theory, previous methodologies, and gaps in the literature. An abstract is a brief and concise summary of a larger written or digital document, a recording, or other work. Students and researchers often include an abstract at the beginning of a research paper or project report as a brief and informative overview of the content, methodology, and results presented in the document to help readers decide if they want to read the entire document.

It is essential for a writer to understand the topic, theoretical perspectives, problems in researching the topic, and major controversies in the topic area of any research project (Adams, Khan, Raeside, & White, 2007). Reading as much of the available literature as possible is the only way to do this. As Ridley (2008) noted, "The literature review is where you identify the theories and previous research which have influenced your choice of research topic and the methodology you are choosing to adopt" (p. 2).

Identifying and Narrowing a Research Topic

Researcher interests in topics may stem from professional exposure to programs, policies, or procedures as well as personal experiences with a particular action or activity. For example, a person who was subjected to child abuse as a youth may now be interested in studying the impact of child abuse on college attendance. He or she may want to investigate the number of formerly abused youth who attended and successfully completed a 4-year degree in colleges in the southern states. Another researcher may have professional experience with the Drug Abuse Resistance Education (DARE) program and be interested in researching the amount of drug use and exposure those who attended the program during 6th grade have in Grades 9 to 12. The interest in this subject may allow for an exploration of the success of the DARE program in deterring drug use in a geographical location.

If the subject for a research paper is not provided by the teacher, students may find that they are overwhelmed by their interest in many topics. The fundamental step, here, is to identify one broad subject and then to restrict the

Table 3.1 Examples of Scholarly Perspectives

	Subject	Narrowed Topic/Scholarly Perspective	Possible Research Topic
Example 1	A student is interested in the design of police cars and the equipment located in the cars	Ergonomics of the police vehicle and the head, neck, shoulder, and hip room provided to officers once technology is incorporated into a police car	Ergonomics and technology in a police vehicle and their physical impact on police officers
Example 2	A student is interested in drug courts	The recidivism rate of adult offenders who attended and completed drug court programs	A quantitative assessment of the recidivism rate of adult offenders who complete drug court programs
Example 3	A student is interested in fake news	The number of fake news stories published on social media in a specific period of time	How widespread are fake news stories on social media? An analysis of fake news stories from 2018 to 2020

interest in that subject to a narrowly defined issue. One should ask, "What is it about that subject that I want to know?" Once the researcher has identified what he or she wants to know, the researcher can frame the project from a scholarly perspective. As identified in Table 3.1, any subject can be investigated from a scholarly perspective if the topic is clearly identified.

Identifying what a researcher wants to know may be easier said than done, however. To do so, the researcher may need to employ several techniques prior to even beginning the research project. The researcher may wish to speak to others, like teachers, friends, or family, to brainstorm the idea and discuss the possible questions he or she may face while researching the topic. The researcher may want to talk to those involved in the activity or action that he or she is interested in. The researcher may want to do a review of the literature found in the library or in Internet searches to see what others have identified as interesting about a subject and what others have found in data analysis with respect to the subject (Lester & Lester, 2005). Using a general search engine, such as Google, is a good way to start researching a topic since it will return the most results. For example, a simple Internet search using the keyword "police body cameras" returns more than 79,000,000 results. Students and researchers, however, cannot effectively evaluate such a volume of search results in the hope of finding the most appropriate data for their study. Once the topic has been identified through a general search, it can be refined by using more specific search terms and an appropriate database. This will reduce the search results significantly, so that students and researchers can more easily identify and evaluate proper sources. Searches can also be limited by using databases and search parameters, which are discussed later in this chapter. Specifying a range of publication dates (e.g., the past 3–5 years) will also limit a search.

A sample search using the EBSCOhost Law and Political Science database reduces the results for "police body cameras" to a more manageable 670 returns. Refining the search to include "privacy" further reduces the results to 38 sources. Although Appendix A is comprehensive, it still remains too broad for a typical literature review (see page 140 for Appendix A). Example 3.1 illustrates seven possible refined topics.

Example 3.1 Possible Topic Areas With Reference Numbers From Appendix A

1. Police wearable video devices

    38, 26, 21, 34, 33, 1, 30, 18, 19, 20, 21, 22

2. Privacy concerns

    2, 4, 6, 8, 10, 13, 16, 24, 23, 26, 27, 29, 31, 37

3. Impact of police cameras

    1, 3, 7, 9, 13, 18, 30

4. Understanding police video camera use

    1, 5, 6, 7, 8, 12, 18, 20, 21, 22

5. Accountability

    3, 6, 7, 8, 10, 18, 23, 24, 26, 27, 29, 30, 32

6. Evidence

    1, 19, 21, 27, 33, 35

7. Legal implications

    1, 3, 10, 11, 17, 22, 32

Exercise 3.1

Practice narrowing a research topic. Select a broad topic, and conduct a library and Internet search. Start with a general search engine (e.g., Google). Then, using the techniques described in this chapter, narrow the topic several times. Continue the process until a manageable number of sources is reached.

Reading source material will increase the student's knowledge in the topic area and lead to other potential source material. Reading source material will also reveal the theoretical perspectives used to identify the type of data needed to answer the research questions (Adams et al., 2007). Additionally, problems with researching the topic area may be identified when reading the literature. For example, Jacobs (1999) observed that no official data exist on criminal offenses committed by police officers. With this knowledge derived from the literature, scholars interested in researching this topic will understand that locating data for their study will be problematic and, if data become available, the value of additional study in this area.

No matter what method is used to narrow the topic, the researcher, ultimately, will need to identify his or her own personal biases about the subject before choosing to begin the research. Because personal biases can influence data-gathering and data analysis processes, the researcher needs to know that he or she can be objective when researching the topic. In other words, the researcher needs to remain distanced from what he or she is studying so that the findings are based on what was studied and not on the researcher's personality, bias, past experiences, or opinions (Payne & Payne, 2004).

Locating Sources

The Internet is an important resource and should be a part of your research plan. With just a few keystrokes, a seemingly endless collection of information can be located. With just a few keystrokes, search engines scan millions of webpages (Hacker, 2006) and return a seemingly limitless amount of information. Students and scholars should be familiar with the various methods available to locate sources and limit the returns to those most relevant to their study. General search techniques are discussed in Chapter 7. This section focuses on locating source material for criminal justice students and scholars.

Using Criminal Justice Databases

Criminal justice databases focus on issues related to crime, law enforcement, prisons and jails, probation and parole, juvenile justice, and the courts. The information located in these databases comes from journals, books, government reports, and private institutional reports. Use these and other related databases when researching a criminal justice topic.

Some databases charge a subscription fee and are not as straightforward to access as general search engines. Most college libraries and some public libraries subscribe to databases that provide unlimited access to scholarly resources not otherwise available on the Internet (Hacker, 2006). Databases like ProQuest, EBSCOhost, and LexisNexis fall into this category. Check the library website, or ask a librarian about how to access these sites. Additional research resources are included in Chapter 6, "The Academic Research Paper."

1. *National Criminal Justice Reference Service* (https://www.ncjrs .gov/App/AbstractDB/AbstractDBSearch.aspx): This free database, operated by the Office of Justice Programs, provides mostly abstracts but also some full-length access for criminal justice topics, with links to data collections and other government programs.

2. *National Archive of Criminal Justice Data* (https://www.icpsr.umich .edu/icpsrweb/content/NACJD/index.html): This archive contains links to more than 2,700 studies of criminal justice data, which can be downloaded for secondary analysis.

3. *Bureau of Justice Statistics* (https://www.bjs.gov/): The Bureau of Justice Statistics (BJS) collects, analyzes, publishes, and disseminates information on crime, criminal offenders, victims of crime, and the operation of justice systems at all levels of government. Primary data are available for download.

4. *Federal Bureau of Investigations Publications* (https://ucr.fbi.gov/ucr-publications): Through this site, the Federal Bureau of Investigations provides data and reports from the Uniform Crime Reports, National Incident-Based Reporting System, and other data collections.

5. *Criminal Justice Abstracts:* Access through EBSCOHost via an institution or local library. Criminal Justice Abstracts is a database for criminal justice and criminology research. It provides cover-to-cover indexing and abstracts for hundreds of journals covering all related subjects, including forensic sciences, corrections, policing, and criminal law and investigation.

6. *JSTOR* (https://www.jstor.org/): JSTOR is a subscription research platform that provides access to millions of journal articles, books, and other primary sources. Students can often access JSTOR through their institution's library.

7. *Other criminal justice databases* (http://libguides.umflint.edu/c.php?g=428962&p=3263967): Students can find an extensive listing of criminal justice databases compiled by the University of Michigan.

Identifying Primary and Secondary Sources

Primary sources include research, publications, reports, interviews, and other original material (Schiffhorst & Schell, 1991). Secondary sources are created with the support of primary sources. Primary sources give a truer sense of the topic than any secondary source could provide (Bombaro, 2012). Collecting data from a primary source, though, can be challenging.

Obtaining primary source data requires conducting individual or focus group interviews, completing survey research, or observing participant behavior, and the process can be both costly and time-consuming. Some primary source data collected by researchers are available on criminal justice databases. For example, a student researching family violence might consult a BJS report. The report is a primary source since it is based on crime statistics collected and analyzed by the BJS and this information is essential to understanding the issue. Students should "locate and use as many primary sources as possible" (Schiffhorst & Schell, 1991, p. 336).

Secondary sources rely on interpreting primary or other secondary sources to support or counter the author's thesis. These include books, scholarly articles, and other documents authored by someone who did not conduct original research or experience the event firsthand (Brown, 2014). Students should evaluate secondary sources carefully for credibility. Companies and organizations often fund research with the intent of a predetermined outcome. Information about evaluating sources is included later in this chapter.

Exercise 3.2

Locate a scholarly article on a topic that interests you. Does the author use primary data or secondary data?

Using Secondary Sources to Locate Primary Sources

Students can benefit from the work of authors who have studied and published criminal justice research on topics similar to theirs. When a source is located, students should carefully read the reference section, paying particular attention to titles that appear to be closely related to their topic. The bibliographic information should be added to the Working Bibliography. Using the author's name and the title of the work, search one of the earlier described databases until the source is located. It is always best to locate a full-text copy of the source. Students can read the full details of the work and evaluate its usefulness to their research essay.

Exercise 3.3

Choose one of the articles found in Exercise 3.1. In the References, find a prominent author or article previously not identified in the exercise. Conduct a search, and locate the article. Repeat the process several times, each time locating new articles or authors. How many new articles or authors did you find? How can adding this information to a paper improve the writer's credibility and the quality of the final paper?

Identifying Classic Studies

It is important to identify the classic studies in a topic area. Classic or landmark studies are those that "change the way we think about criminal justice topics, generated considerable amount of other research, and have had a major influence on the operation of the criminal justice system" (Thistlethwaite & Wooldredge, 2010, p. xix). Our knowledge of the criminal justice system is based on these studies, and they provide a rich foundation for students and researchers to understand the context of future criminal justice research (Thistlethwaite & Wooldredge, 2010).

Be alert for certain keywords that identify classic studies, such as *classic, foundational, famous, definitive, groundbreaking,* or *seminal.* The following examples demonstrate how a keyword can identify a classic study:

1. "This *landmark* experiment found that traditional routine patrol in marked police cars does not appear to affect the level of crime" (National Police Foundation, 2016).

2. "This view was supported by the findings of the *pioneering* Minneapolis, Minnesota domestic violence arrest experiment (also called the Minneapolis Spouse Abuse Experiment), the first controlled experiment in the use of arrest for any offense, which found a substantial specific deterrent effect in a sample of 314 cases" (Sherman, Schmidt, Rogan, & Smith, 1992, p. 138).

3. "The *major* studies examining the issue of patrol-unit numbers have attempted to discern differences between solo patrols and two-officer patrols regarding the type of activities undertaken, the quantity of tasks completed within a given unit of time (e.g., one shift period), response time, and the quality of the task resolution" (Wilson & Brewer, 1992, p. 444).

4. "These *emergent* perspectives played an important role in legitimating the decision of many academic criminologists and juridical policymakers to declare rehabilitation fully bankrupt. Most *noteworthy* was Robert Martinson's (1974:25) conclusion that 'the rehabilitative efforts that have been reported so far have had no appreciable effect on recidivism'" (Andrews et al., 1990, p. 370).

5. "Few ideas have become more influential than 'broken windows'" (Sampson & Raudenbush, 2004, p. 319).

Pre-reading Source Material

Pre-reading is a strategy successful students and scholars often use to help them focus and concentrate on important material in a text. In source material, researchers hope to discover information that will expand their knowledge of the topic, guide their choice of research methodology, inform their current study, and lead to other instructive source studies. Pre-reading includes listing keywords and concepts, identifying successful and unsuccessful study methodologies, and learning about findings that may be valuable to the student's research. Given the quantity of potential sources found in a search, students should quickly and efficiently determine if the identified source material is useful to their study. This can be done by scanning the source material. Since social science research is written in a specific format, students can focus on several easily located areas of a source paper before reading the entire text. Special focus should be given to these key areas in any research paper:

1. The title

2. The abstract and/or introduction

3. The first two or three sentences of each bolded heading and subheading

4. The first two or three sentences of other subheadings

5. Any tables, graphs, charts, or data presented in a labeled and titled box

6. The methodologies used
   a. The sample/population
   b. The sampling method
   c. Whether quantitative or qualitative
   d. The method of analysis
   e. Methodological strengths and weaknesses
7. The findings
8. The discussion section
   a. Limitations
9. The bibliography or references section

Evaluating Sources

All source material should be evaluated thoroughly since anyone can post information to the Web. Not using a plausible source can discredit an essay and the writer. According to Kirszner and Mandell (2011), students should ask four questions when evaluating sources:

1. Is the source *respected*? Peer-reviewed, scholarly articles are valued much more than general readership articles. Likewise, a major news publication, like *The Wall Street Journal* or *The New York Times*, is considered a more dependable source than an independent newspaper.

2. Is the source *reliable*? Reliable sources depend on factual, documented information that supports the thesis. In a reliable source, the author will include source citations that can be checked for accuracy.

3. Is the source *current*? Current sources provide information relevant to the topic. There is no standard for how old a publication might be yet still remain current. A technology article could be outdated in a year or less, while information on community policing from the 1980s might be current.

4. Is the author of the source *credible*? What other publications has the author written, and have they been cited by other researchers? Is the author employed by a company or foundation that suggests a particular bias?

Exercise 3.4

Evaluate a source used in a previous exercise. Is the source respected, reliable, current, and credible? Based on the evaluation, could the source be used in a research paper?

Organizing the Review

The literature review should follow a general organization principle of at least three elements: (1) an introduction section; (2) the body section, containing the discussion of sources; and (3) a conclusion or recommendations section (University of North Carolina at Chapel Hill, 2019).

Previous studies may have a qualitative or quantitative design, and this design affects the organization of the literature review. According to Denney and Tewksbury (2013), reviews of qualitative studies focus on important themes and how the research question was studied previously. Literature reviews for quantitative studies discuss the previous literature, specific variables, and the analytic methods used. They focus on the research methods—both what has been used in previous studies and new methods that represent advances in research design. The review may also be organized chronologically to demonstrate improvements in research methods or technology, or thematically to focus sections of the review on specific topics (University of North Carolina at Chapel Hill, 2019).

Writing the Review

As with any writing project, the literature review deserves the author's best effort and writing skills. The review is written in a narrative format, in the past tense, and in complete sentences that are grammatically correct and devoid of punctuation and spelling errors. Source citations follow standard American Psychological Association format for both in-text and bibliographic references. The review should be written for a general audience, without slang or jargon. Example 3.2 is an example of a literature review. Since Example 3.2 is a writing sample, references are not included in the list.

The University of North Carolina at Chapel Hill (2019) Writing Center recommends the following guidelines for writing a literature review:

1. *Use evidence:* Support the interpretation of the source with other sources to demonstrate validity.

2. *Be selective:* Use only the most important points that focus on methodology, themes, or chronology.

3. *Use quotations sparingly:* Some short quotes are acceptable, but the review does not lend itself to an in-depth analysis or detailed quoting of the source.

4. *Avoid summarizing the source:* Sources should be used to convey and support the writer's ideas. Sources should not be used as the sole text of the review.

5. *Paraphrase accurately:* Represent the source material accurately, and refer to the source when discussing information that is not your original idea. Avoid plagiarism.

What Is a Literature Review?

A literature review is an analysis of significant sources to support the writer's ideas on a research topic, theory, previous methodologies, and gaps in the literature. Important reasons for writing a literature review include demonstrating the author's knowledge of the topic and previously written studies, establishing the writer's study within the framework of prior research, and establishing the need for the writer's study. Students and researchers should keep in mind several key elements when writing the review.

1. *Pre-read the material for efficiency:* Using pre-reading strategies, students and researchers should identify the most timely sources. Timeliness refers to the article's relevance to the writer's topic, not the date when the source was written. Source articles written within the past 10 years are accepted by most professors as timely, but studies written even 50 or more years ago can be considered timely. For example, the president's Commission on Law Enforcement and Administration of Justice report, written in 1967, could be considered timely today for studies on juvenile delinquency, police management, community-based corrections, and strategies of crime control. Similarly, August Vollmer, considered the father of American policing, wrote *The Police and Modern Society: Plain Talk Based on Practical Experience* in 1936. The text can still be purchased today and is considered by many as a foundational work in policing. Although using outdated source material may be beneficial in a historical context, including material in a literature review that is not considered timely and relevant can be evidence of poor research skills.

2. *Organize the review:* Students should organize the literature review to help readers understand the important topics identified in previous studies. The literature review can be organized based on the research methodology, theory, chronology, or theme of earlier works. Reviews organized according to research methodology should focus on the use of qualitative or quantitative methods. Quantitative studies are based on statistical analytical methods, while qualitative studies focus on themes identified by the researcher.

3. *Analyze, don't summarize:* A common mistake in writing literature reviews is to simply summarize earlier works. A summary provides no more information to the reader than if the reader had read the article firsthand. The analysis provided in a literature review should assure the reader that previous studies employed appropriate methodologies, identified methodological flaws or limitations that affected the findings, and communicated significant study findings that supported

the research hypotheses of earlier studies. A good analysis demonstrates the need for additional study and allows students to frame their study in such a way that it builds on and adds to the previous scholarship.

4. *Use evidence to support claims:* In a literature review, claims made by the writer must be supported by evidence from previous studies. Scholarly research is based on knowledge, and the process of analyzing earlier works and writing a literature review demonstrates a student's understanding of the topic. Declarative statements and claims of fact should be supported by source material that is cited so that readers can verify the information presented in the paper.

5. *Identify theory:* Many researchers frame their research within the context of criminological or other social science theory. Prominent criminology theories include anomie, strain, social learning, social disorganization, labeling, rational choice, and others. The analysis of source material should identify the theoretical perspectives and their relevance to the current study.

6. *Identify previous research methodologies:* A well-written literature review seeks to identify research methodologies that have been used successfully in the past as well as those that demonstrated limited effectiveness. Doing so demonstrates the writer's knowledge of research methods. It also supports the use of a past design in the student's current study or justifies the need for applying an alternative methodology.

7. *Identify gaps in the literature:* A foundational purpose of a literature review is to justify the need for the current study. The literature review does this by acknowledging the existing knowledge on a topic and identifying an area that would expand or improve on this body of knowledge.

8. *Acknowledge dissenting views:* In rhetorical terms, a research study is an argumentative paper. The writer proposes a thesis and offers evidence in support. Acknowledging dissenting views does several things: It demonstrates that the writer is not one-sided and has considered alternatives before reaching a conclusion (Harvey, 1999).

The literature review is a critical piece of a research project. Reading the available literature will improve students' knowledge of the topic and may allow them to speak to topic experts. Perhaps most rewarding, though, is the feeling of inclusion derived from the connection between other scholars' work and your own. As noted by Adams et al. (2007), writing the literature review introduces students to an academic community as someone "who can speak and write with confidence and authority on a specific research problem" (p. 39). A sample literature review is provided in Example 3.2.

CALEA and Professionalism

The concept of professionalism in policing can be traced to the early 19th century, when visionaries like August Vollmer and Orlando Wilson led the movement toward police professionalism. Vollmer is recognized as the principal author of the professional model of policing, which includes a deep involvement in the community (Carte & Carte, 1975), and in 1921, he was named president of the International Association of Chiefs of Police (2014)—one of CALEA's four founding organizations. When he was chief of the Chicago Police Department, Wilson implemented his model of police management, which emphasized organization autonomy, efficiency, and accountability (Hassell et al., 2003; Kelling & Wycoff, 2001). Both men contributed to a foundation for professionalism in policing, and on its establishment, CALEA's goals included establishing standards designed to increase agency professionalism.

Several studies recognize CALEA's contribution in promoting professional law enforcement (Baker, 1995; Bizzack, 1993; Crowder, 1998; Langer, 1995). Specifically, Baker (1995) notes that the differences brought about through the credentialing process clearly differentiate CALEA agencies from their nonaccredited peers; Cheurprakobkit (1996) suggests that accreditation is the benchmark of professionalism; Falzarano (1999) writes that accreditation represents the first step in establishing law enforcement professionalism; McCabe and Fajardo (2001) conclude that accreditation is an avenue to achieving professionalism in law enforcement; Trautman (1988) includes accreditation as a characteristic of law enforcement professionalism; and Langer (1995) suggests that accreditation allows an agency to demonstrate that it is a professional organization. These studies suggest that by complying with CALEA's 480 standards accredited agencies go about the business of the profession in clearly identifiable and measurable ways that set them apart from nonaccredited agencies.

Citizen Complaints

In 2008, about 40 million people aged 16 years or older had at least one face-to-face contact with the police (Eith & Durose, 2011). While the vast majority of citizens (89.7%) felt that the police acted properly, 574,000 reported that the police threatened or used force against them, and 417,000 (1.4%) reported that they felt the force was excessive (Eith & Durose, 2011). Although the number of police–citizen contacts has steadily declined, the percentage of complaints related to the use of excessive force has remained constant at about 1.5% since 2002 (Eith & Durose, 2011).

There are many factors that influence complaints filed against police officers, but most often they result from street-level actions on the part of individual officers (Christensen, 2001; Dauler & Romano, 1993; Vaughn et al., 2001). Research suggests that a White, male officer under the age of 30 years, with less than 5 years' experience, and assigned to uniform patrol is most likely to generate complaints (Johnson, 1998; Steven et al., 2001). There is some evidence that the number of complaints is tied to officer productivity, since officers who make more arrests and issue more citations generate more complaints (Brandl et al., 2001, Hassell & Archbold, 2010; Lersch, 2002). Eith and Durose (2011) reported that most of those who experienced police force felt that the amount of force used was excessive

(76%) or that the police acted improperly (84%). Many of these incidents involved the police making threats or shouting, but 83% of excessive force incidents involved physical force (pushing, hitting, kicking, use of a chemical agent, or use of an electronic control device) (Eith & Durose, 2011). Forty percent of the recipients of force were arrested, and 19% were injured during the incident, while 14% reported that they had filed a complaint against the police (Eith & Durose, 2011).

Hickman (2006) found that in 2002 the nation's police agencies had received 26,000 citizen complaints alleging excessive use of force by police officers. Durose, Schmitt, and Langan (2005) recorded complaints filed not only with the officer's employing agency but also with a civilian complaint review board, the local prosecutor, the court, or another government agency and found that a total of 101,600 complaints were filed against officers for excessive use of force. Hickman (2006) reported that about 8% of complaints of excessive use of force are substantiated, which is less than the substantiation rate for other types of complaints (Griswold, 1994).

The interpretation of these numbers, however, is complex and prone to both underreporting and overreporting (Lersch, 1999). Some citizens may define misconduct more broadly than agency policy, and others may be dissatisfied with the officer's conduct or the outcome of an investigation (Lersch, 1999). Some studies suggest that low complaint rates may alternately indicate confidence and trust in an agency (Adams, 1995) or the presence of intake processes that discourage citizens from filing complaints (Pate et al., 1993). Some may lack confidence in the agency, find the process intimidating, or wish to not draw attention to their criminal past (Lersch, 1999). A high number of sustained complaints, however, may suggest misconduct. Other studies suggest that race and socioeconomic status determine the number of complaints. African Americans are overrepresented in the volume of complaints filed (Kessler, 1999), but this may be due to a large number of force incidents occurring in minority and poor neighborhoods (Adams, 1995). Still others file frivolous complaints in an effort to have charges dropped (Lersch, 1998) or to leverage the courts (Adams, 1995).

While the LEMAS data do not include the previously mentioned dimensions, they include the following additional factors that may influence the rate at which complaints are filed and their outcome. A number of studies suggest that agencies that make improvements in the complaint process, such as accepting complaints by phone, increasing the number of locations where a complaint may be filed, or involving citizens in the complaint review process, experience a higher volume of complaints but sustain fewer claims of malpractice (Adams, 1995; Kessler, 1999; Walker & Bumphus, 1992; Worrall, 2002). Worrall (2002) examined the impact of four organizational factors on the frequency of complaints: (1) trained internal affairs investigators, (2) external citizen review, (3) operating an early-warning system, and (4) electronic complaint databases); they found operating an early-warning system significant. CALEA (2013a) standards require that agencies operate an early-warning system as a means of identifying potential problem employees. Hickman (2006) reported that the involvement of a citizen complaint review board, the use of an internal affairs unit, the use of an early-warning system, the use of computerized files to record complaints, and the presence of collective bargaining increased the rate of citizen complaints. Police union contracts, however, have been reported to inhibit the investigation of misconduct (Walker, 2006). Because of these larger global issues, complaint numbers

(Continued)

(Continued)

must be viewed holistically rather than simply examining the number of complaints.

The Lack of CALEA Diffusion

Obtaining accredited status is a process in which very few agencies choose to participate. Since its creation almost 35 years ago, CALEA has awarded accredited status to just 623 U.S. state, local, and national law enforcement agencies—a mere 3% of the nation's 18,000 policing agencies and a number that has remained static for the past 10 years. Stated another way, 97% of police managers have chosen not to participate in a voluntary process that can be arduous, costly, and labor intensive (Baker, 1995; Carter & Sapp, 1994; Cheurprakobkit, 1996; Falzarano, 1999; McCabe & Fajardo, 2001).

Most of the nation's largest agencies are noticeably missing from CALEA's membership. The nation's six largest police departments are not accredited, and of the 10 largest agencies, 8 are not accredited. By size, these nonaccredited agencies include New York City P.D., Chicago P.D., Los Angeles P.D., Philadelphia P.D., Houston P.D., Washington D.C. Metro Police, Dallas P.D., and Detroit P.D. Of the nation's 10 largest sheriff's offices, only 1 agency (Broward County, Florida, Sheriff's Office) is accredited. The level of participation begs the questions whether accreditation works and what tangible benefits it provides to law enforcement, citizens, and public managers.

Assessing the Impact of CALEA Accreditation

Studies evaluating the impact of CALEA voluntary credentialing are mixed. In their analysis, McCabe and Fajardo (2001) identified several differences between accredited and nonaccredited agencies, including in field training hours, minimum education requirements for starting officers, policies for drug testing sworn applicants, the operation of a drug unit, and the operation of a child abuse unit. Accredited agencies were more likely to use polygraph exams and pre-employment drug testing (Baker, 1995). CALEA accredited agencies are most often located in the South and are less likely to have unions (Alpert & MacDonald, 2001). Bizzack (1993) suggested that accredited agencies experience increased calls for service, crime clearance rates, and community confidence and have fewer citizen complaints.

But Carter and Sapp (1994) observed that the chiefs of nonaccredited agencies are uncertain about the value of accreditation, and Sykes (1994) reported that CALEA accreditation fails to considerably change an agency. Skolnick and Fyfe (1994) added that most CALEA standards lack substantive content, requiring only that the agency have a policy but leaving the content details to the agency. Cordner and Williams (1998) suggested that accreditation standards emphasize process over outcome and have little impact on the quality and nature of the services delivered. Recent studies examining outcome measures have suggested that accreditation has no impact on operational effectiveness (Teodoro & Hughes, 2012), case clearance rates (Doerner & Doerner, 2012), reducing incidents involving the use of force (Alpert & MacDonald, 2001), and the frequency or severity of lawsuits (Hougland & Mesloh, 2005).

The current study seeks to expand on previous studies that identified the key characteristics of CALEA accredited agencies (Baker, 1995; Bizzack, 1993; Cheurprakobkit, 1996; Crowder, 1998; Langer, 1995). Specifically, Bizzack (1993) surveyed 325 CALEA accredited agencies and identified decreased citizen complaints as one such characteristic. Using the data provided in the 2007 LEMAS survey, we attempt to determine the influence of CALEA accreditation on the volume of citizen complaints regarding the use of force, and on the outcome of the complaint investigations, from a national sample of state and local law enforcement agencies.

We distinguish CALEA accreditation for several reasons. First, as the first national accrediting body, CALEA stands as the model for law enforcement accreditation. Its four founding bodies offer its standards a level of legitimacy unparalleled in state programs. Second, at least some state programs predominately replicate CALEA standards, while others are entirely distinct. Florida's process, for example, duplicates CALEA standards, with the exception of 81 standards (Commission for Florida Law Enforcement Accreditation, Inc., 2014). Other state programs are completely different from CALEA. Washington's program, for example, was created in 1976—3 years before CALEA was formed. Its standards are based mostly on state and federal law (Washington Association of Sheriffs and Police Chiefs, 2014). An analysis including state agencies, then, would likely either (a) include processes that are highly correlated or (b) muddy the findings with a number of accredited agencies complying with dissimilar standards.

Source: The full document can be read at https://journals.sagepub.com/doi/full/10.1177/0032258X16 671030.

Writing an Abstract

An abstract is a brief and concise summary of a larger written or digital document, a recording, or other work. The abstract is written when a research project is completed. Students and researchers often include an abstract at the beginning of a research paper or project as a brief introduction to the project. It is written in the past tense in one paragraph of no more than 300 words, although the type of abstract may require more or fewer words. The purpose of an abstract is to provide the reader with a brief and informative overview of the content, methodology, and results contained in the document and to help readers decide if they want to read the entire document. It is important for students and researchers to write a complete and thorough abstract since it may be the only section of the paper or article read by others.

Types of Abstracts

An abstract can be written by a student evaluating research for use in a paper or by researchers summarizing their own study. The following general types of abstracts are typically used for academic papers, conference presentations, and publications.

Critical Abstract

A critical abstract evaluates a work's benefit to another study. In addition to including the purpose, methods, and results, a critical abstract includes an analysis of the work. Professors sometimes assign a critical abstract so that students have a record of their research and its benefit to the student's paper. Due to the analysis included in the critical abstract, this abstract is typically about 400 words (University of Southern California Libraries, 2019).

Descriptive Abstract

A descriptive abstract briefly summarizes the information found in a work. It does not evaluate the work in any way. It does include the purpose, methods, and scope of the report but not the results, conclusions, and recommendations (Purdue OWL, n.d.). Descriptive abstracts are typically just 100, or fewer, words in length (University of Southern California Libraries, 2019). The reader must decide if the subject is interesting enough or of sufficient value to read the entire report.

Informative Abstract

The informative abstract embodies the entire work. It includes all the information found in a descriptive abstract, but it also contains a discussion of the results, implications, and recommendations of the study. Informative abstracts are written by researchers to help readers decide if they should read the entire study. This abstract is typically about 250 to 300 words long (University of Southern California Libraries, 2019).

Writing Style

Students and researchers should follow the basic concepts for writing well when writing an abstract. Write in complete sentences, using specific words and concepts from the full document. Address the main points of the document, and write in the active voice. Write in a general style so that readers not familiar with the topic can easily understand the abstract. Avoid using jargon and acronyms since the abstract does not provide sufficient space to explain their meaning. Samples of abstracts are provided in Examples 3.3 and 3.4.

Abstract Elements

Like any piece of writing, a well-written abstract is organized to help the reader understand its content. A well-written abstract includes six elements (adapted from ERIC, n.d.; University of Southern California Libraries, 2019):

1. *Purpose:* Describes the objective and hypothesis of the document

2. *Methods:* Describes the research design, data, and analysis methods

3. *Results:* Describes the findings of the analysis

4. *Interpretations:* Provides a brief summary of the reader's understanding of the work

5. *Implications:* Suggests how the results will have an impact on the literature or on policy and makes suggestions for future studies

6. *Additional materials:* Identifies tables, graphs, and other materials included in the full document

Example 3.3 Sample Quantitative Abstract

Accreditation in Police Agencies: Does External Quality Assurance Reduce Citizen Complaints?

Accreditation suggests that an organization has met standards of quality through extensive self-study and external review. This study examines the influence of Commission on Accreditation for Law Enforcement Agencies (CALEA) accreditation on citizen complaints. The authors identified the accredited status of the law enforcement agencies included in the 2007 LEMAS report as CALEA accredited or nonaccredited, resulting in a final sample size for this study of 628 agencies (CALEA accredited = 314, nonaccredited = 314).

The study uses an experimental design and a negative binomial regression. The findings suggest that no difference exists between CALEA-accredited agencies and nonaccredited agencies in (a) the total number of complaints received and (b) the number of sustained citizen complaints. The study suggests that CALEA accreditation has no impact on the volume of citizen complaints an agency may receive or the investigatory outcome of those complaints, and provides insight for future citizen complaint research.

Source: The full document can be read at https://journals.sagepub.com/doi/full/10.1177/0032258X16671030.

Example 3.4 Sample Qualitative Abstract

Consolidation of Local Government Agencies: Does Florida's Fiscal Crisis Merit Merging Law Enforcement Agencies?

The traditional model of municipal, county, and state government has led to duplication and inefficiencies of police services. In many areas, the delivery of police services is duplicated by city, county, and state agencies that often perform similar or identical functions. Many agencies are considering consolidation as a means of reducing costs. This study examines the historical effectiveness of consolidating local law enforcement agencies and suggests three policy alternatives.

A consolidated government is one in which local governing entities formally create a single government entity that assumes responsibility for both city and county. In counties that support numerous police departments and a sheriff's office, proponents of consolidation suggest that it makes good fiscal sense to operate one law enforcement agency rather than a multitude of independent agencies that all perform essentially the same police function.

Consolidation efforts have been implemented in Florida. Most notable of these efforts are the Miami and Jacksonville models. Alternatively, many large agencies have implemented a scaled-down version of consolidation, sometimes called regionalization, by providing contract services to smaller communities within their jurisdiction. Other, smaller agencies have entered partnerships to share facilities and resources. The goal of each of these programs was to reduce cost, eliminate wasteful duplication of services, and improve efficiencies.

Consolidation of local law enforcement agencies has seen mixed reviews. Empirical studies have consistently failed to find economies of scale due to such consolidation. Policy implications include standardized pay, pensions, uniforms, firearms, vehicles, and other equipment.

Source: Author created.

CHAPTER SUMMARY

Writing literature reviews and abstracts is an important part of writing college research assignments and peer-reviewed articles. A literature review is a summary of what the literature says about a specific topic (Purdue OWL, 2018d), and an abstract is a summary of any work. A well-written literature review demonstrates the writer's knowledge of the topic, establishes the need for the research, and justifies the research methodology. This chapter discusses the writing process and key elements of a literature review. The purpose of an abstract is to provide the reader with a brief and informative overview of the content, methodology, and results contained in the document and to help readers decide if they want to read the entire document. It is important for students and researchers to write a complete and thorough abstract since it may be the only section of the paper or article read by others.

QUESTIONS FOR CONSIDERATION

1. In what ways should a literature review establish the need for a research project? Why is it important for the literature review to do this?

2. How can a writer address the gaps in the literature identified in a literature review?

3. How can a writer establish the need for a research methodology used in a research paper or peer-reviewed article?

4. What is the purpose of an abstract, and how does it encourage the reader to read the full paper?

Research Designs, Data Collection Methods, and Data Analysis

This chapter is not designed to take the place of a research methods course. It is only a brief discussion of the concepts a researcher will write about in the methods section of a research paper. The methodology section of a research paper explains the research design and the procedures implemented in a study. In this portion of a paper, researchers describe why their chosen research design was the best one to use in their study and the advantages and disadvantages of the methodology. The setting, participants, and hypotheses, and any applicable coding schemes are also described. Additionally, researchers will explain why their method of data collection was the most beneficial and how the data will be analyzed with statistical formulas.

This chapter will describe how to begin writing a research paper, and quantitative, qualitative, and mixed methods methodologies. Methods of data collection, such as surveys and interviews, will also be described. Field observations and experiments will be briefly mentioned, and the chapter will end with a very general discussion of data analysis. How to write about the setting, subjects, and coding design, and other topics in a methods section will be briefly explained at the end of the chapter.

How to Begin

When writing a research paper, the researcher should begin with a clear outline and understanding of the topic. As discussed in Chapter 3, narrowing the topic to something one cares about and is willing to invest time and effort into understanding is a key step in writing a research paper. A research paper is different from an anecdotal or opinion-based paper in that the author's ideas should be supported by collective evidence and other research from experts in the field (Lester & Lester, 2005). The writer should investigate the topic using various methods of investigation, from library or Internet research to surveys and interviews of those most familiar with the topic, and analyze the findings to support or deny the author's and other researchers' opinions of the topic. For example, a doctoral student who is also a police officer may write a research dissertation using interviews with women who have escaped sex trafficking rings to determine how the women became involved in the trade to begin with. The student would initially develop hypotheses, which are assertions of why women become involved in the sex trafficking trade, founded in the literature or from personal experiences of the student as a police officer working in this field. Then, the student would locate these women through his job as a police officer and hold one-on-one interviews with them regarding their involvement. Finally, the student would analyze the interviews to see if there were common reasons provided by the women on why they joined the sex trade. The commonalities and differences in their responses would be discussed in the research paper along with how this research project contributes to the literature available on the topic, or in criminology in general.

When deciding to write a research paper, a student will most likely want to identify the reason(s) for the study. Perhaps he or she is interested in discovering new information on a topic or in exploring a subject not much is known about. The student may also have a goal of explaining a phenomenon. Lester and Lester (2005, pp. 2–3) claimed that research accomplishes five basic goals:

1. *Teaching methods of discovery:* Research allows a student to probe, through surveys, interviews, or observations, a complex subject and to identify what he or she may already know or what others may know about the subject.

2. *Teaching investigative skills:* Research allows a student to use a variety of sources, like the library or the Internet, to find reliable and credible information about a subject and to use additional methods of investigation, like surveys, interviews, and observation or laboratory work, to explore the subject.

3. *Teaching critical thinking:* Research allows a student to use information literacy skills to determine what is useful information and to disregard unfounded literature.

4. *Teaching logic:* Research allows a student to use reasoning to judge the issues surrounding a subject and to interpret the data collected while reading, observing, interviewing, or testing.

5. *Teaching the basic ingredients of argument:* Research allows a student to make a claim and support it through evidence gathered during the research process.

Research, then, is an essential step in developing a scholarly perspective. It requires a well-developed study based on scientific inquiry and the sharing of information with others (Lester & Lester, 2005). In developing a study, a student will begin by considering a topic, researching the topic to determine what is already known, developing hypotheses, and identifying the methodology and methods that will be used to explore the topic. Finally, the student will identify potential data analysis procedures that will be used to analyze the gathered information and the potential implications of the findings in relation to practice, policy, or theory in the field of study.

Developing a Research Question

What to study is derived out of knowledge of the topic. In-depth knowledge of a topic will generate a few questions that can be used to determine if the topic should and can be studied and to support the need for the research study (Farrugia, Petrisor, Farrokhyar, & Bhandari, 2010). While learning about a topic, one may find that there is a lack of a specific knowledge base on a subject and/or there are mixed results about an area of focus within a topic. If one is studying body cameras in corrections, for example, one may find that there is a lack of information on whether they change the nature of interactions between correctional officers and inmates. Or when studying ethics in policing, one may find that a specific entrance examination used in new hire processes produces mixed results on the ethical standards used by those seeking entrance into the policing profession. These weaknesses can lead to the development of a new study that seeks to fill the void in the literature or to find the errors in the entrance exam that may be leading to mixed testing results. Being aware of current trends and technological advances that may affect a field is also beneficial when trying to develop a research question and hypotheses (Farrugia et al., 2010).

All research questions should be developed at the beginning of a study (Farrugia et al., 2010), and focus should be placed on a primary research question. Research questions can be developed in very similar ways to how one narrows a topic (discussed in Chapter 3), including through library database searches, Internet searches, discussions with experts in the field or those involved in the activity or action of interest, focus groups, and so on. Regardless of how one develops a research question, the primary research question should be the focus of the study and used to design the plan of the study. Any additional questions, or secondary research questions, should not overshadow the primary research question. When adding additional research questions, one should keep in mind that they may add to the complexity of the study design and the statistical analysis that will need to be conducted on the data gathered (Farrugia et al., 2010). As stated by Farrugia et al. (2010), "A well-defined and specific research question is more likely to help guide us in making decisions about study design and population and subsequently what data will be collected and analyzed" (p. 278). So, when possible, a researcher may wish to develop only a single, primary research question to focus on in the study design.

The primary research question should be clearly stated in the introduction of the paper. In general, the research question should state the population to be studied, the methodology and methods to be used to gather the data, and any conditional factors that are relevant to the study (Farrugia et al., 2010). It is also standard practice to acknowledge the need for the study (or its importance), such as filling a gap in the literature, assessing the effectiveness of a program, and so on, when identifying the research question. This provides the reader with a clear understanding of what the researcher is doing, to whom, how, and why.

Exercise 4.1

Suppose you are interested in studying the smoking habits of high school students. Write a possible research question, including the population to be studied, the methodology, and the data collection method you will use to gather the data.

The FINER approach. Hulley, Cummings, Browner, Grady, and Newman (2007) have suggested using the FINER criteria—*feasible, interesting, novel, ethical,* and *relevant*—when creating a research question. The FINER approach recommends using these five conditions in the development of a thorough research question:

1. *Feasibility*—identifying a population one can actually access, doing research that is affordable and that the researcher has time to complete, focusing on a topic that the researcher has adequate expertise in, and choosing a topic and population that are manageable

2. *Having interest*—choosing a topic and question that, if addressed, would be intriguing to the researcher, peers, and the scientific community

3. *Being novel*—choosing a topic and question that expand on the literature already available on a subject, confirm findings that already exist on a topic, or refute previous findings in the literature

4. *Exercising ethics*—creating a study that the institutional review board (IRB) and the government will approve and that exercises the ethics of a professional association or discipline

5. *Being relevant*—focusing on a timely project and topic that are appealing to the larger scientific community or to a profession, and have implications for policy, practice, or theory, and/or future research (Farrugia et al., 2010)

According to Farrugia et al. (2010), the FINER approach emphasizes the important aspects of the research question in general.

The PICO method. There is another evidence-based practice in research question development that focuses on the information to be included in a research question (Heneghan & Badenoch, 2002). This is known as the PICO method. This method consists of a focus on identifying the population to be studied, the intervention to be used or that will potentially influence the findings, the comparison group or the comparable intervention, and the outcome of interest. Often included in the PICO method is timing (PICO(T)). Timing is the time frame to which the study will be limited (Heneghan & Badenoch, 2002). Farrugia et al. (2010) suggested that

> the PICOT approach helps generate a question that aids in constructing the framework of the study and subsequently in protocol development by alluding to the inclusion and exclusion criteria and identifying the groups of [participants] to be included. Knowing the specific population of interest, intervention (and comparator) and outcome of interest may also help the researcher identify an appropriate outcome measurement tool. (p. 279)

The more defined the population is, the easier it is for the researcher to apply and generalize the findings. Additionally, a clearly defined study population that has inclusion and exclusion criteria can reduce bias and increase the internal validity of the study (Farrugia et al., 2010).

Exercise 4.2

Using the FINER method, develop a research project and potential research question. Be sure to identify how the study is feasible, interesting, novel, ethical, and relevant.

In summary, a researcher should devote appropriate time and attention, as well as resources, to the development of a research question. A poorly developed research question could result in a wrong choice of study methodology and methods as well as hamper any significant findings in the field of study. A poorly designed research question could also lead to bias and issues in validity and reliability (Farrugia et al., 2010). Any chance of publication of the findings could also be lost. However, a well-designed research question can lead to significant findings in the discipline, changes in a policy or practice used in a profession, and potential generalizability to a larger population outside the study. Thus, it is imperative for a researcher to develop a research question that is answerable and relevant (Farrugia et al., 2010).

Exercise 4.3

Using the PICO(T) method, write a research question that focuses on violence in schools. Be sure to identify the population, intervention, comparison group (or comparison intervention), potential outcome, and timeline.

Developing a Hypothesis

A study is driven by a good research question and hypothesis, not by the data collected. Both the hypothesis and the research question should be created prior to beginning any data collection (Farrugia et al., 2010). Although this seems to be a backward concept, one should consider the fact that a researcher is seeking an answer, not a question, when completing a research study. In other words, using data to create the question allows for bias and findings identified by chance rather than sound best practices and scientific methodology (Farrugia et al., 2010). Luckmann (2001) argued that it is only after the research question and the hypothesis are developed that a researcher can identify the main elements of the study, such as the sampling strategy for the population, the intervention, the comparison group (if applicable), and the potential outcome. This, then, allows for the testing, data collection, data analysis, and discussion.

A hypothesis "requires a careful examination to prove its validity" (Lester & Lester, 2005, p. 25). Although, sometimes the careful examination does not support the hypothesis. Denying a hypothesis can be just as significant as supporting a hypothesis. Take, for example, the researcher who was studying the DARE program. The researcher may have been interested in determining if the DARE program reduced drug use and abuse among 9th to 12th graders. The hypothesis may have suggested that drug use and abuse would be lower among those 9th to 12th graders who completed the DARE program as 6th graders when compared with those who did not attend a DARE program. However, the researcher may find after surveying 9th- to 12th-grade students that there was no difference in drug use and abuse between those who completed the program and those who did not. In this case, showing that the data did not support the hypothesis is just as significant as showing that the data supported it. It may well be that the DARE program is ineffective or that it should be offered at a later grade level, it needs additional interventions (e.g., parental involvement), the curriculum needs revision, or another program would be more beneficial in reducing drug use and abuse among high schoolers. A finding like this could affect policy and practice.

Writing hypotheses. "The purpose of hypothesis testing is to make an inference about the population of interest on the basis of a random sample taken from that population" (Farrugia et al., 2010, p. 280). So a researcher should write a hypothesis as nondirectional, or as a null hypothesis. What this means is that the researcher is looking for no statistically significant difference between one intervention as compared with another. Using the DARE example again, the researcher would write the null hypothesis as follows: *There is no statistically significant difference in drug use and abuse among 9th to 12th graders who completed the DARE program in the 6th grade as compared with 9th to 12th graders who did not complete the DARE program.* Notice that, just as with the research question, the population is identified (9th to 12th graders), the intervention is identified (DARE program), the comparison group is identified (9th to 12th graders who did not attend the DARE program), and the outcome is identified (no statistically significant difference in drug use and abuse). Once the null hypothesis, which is the hypothesis to be tested in the data analysis, is written, the researcher can write an alternative hypothesis. This is the hypothesis the researcher believes may occur. If the DARE program researcher believes that the DARE program will change drug use and abuse behaviors, he or she would write the alternative hypothesis as follows: *There is a statistically significant difference in drug use and abuse among 9th to 12th graders who completed the DARE program in the 6th grade as compared with 9th to 12th graders who did not complete the DARE program.* The data collected are then used to determine which hypothesis is correct. If there is a statistically significant difference in the drug use and abuse levels of 9th to 12th graders who completed the DARE program as compared with those who did not, the researcher would reject the null hypothesis and support the alternative hypothesis (i.e., drug use and abuse levels are either higher or lower among those who completed the DARE program). The absence of a statistically significant difference would result in accepting the null hypothesis (i.e., both groups are using and abusing drugs at about the same levels) and rejecting the alternative hypothesis. "In other words, hypothesis testing confirms or refutes the statement that the observed findings did not occur by chance alone but rather occurred because there was a true difference in outcomes" (Farrugia et al., 2010, p. 280).

Develop a null hypothesis and an alternative hypothesis for a study focused on the presence of school resource officers in relation to criminal behaviors among students in elementary schools.

Although there are many intricacies to hypothesis development and testing that are well beyond the scope of this chapter and are provided in a course designed to teach research methods, this book would be remiss if it did not mention directional hypotheses. Researchers can develop one-sided or two-sided hypotheses. A one-sided hypothesis provides a direction (Farrugia et al., 2010). A two-sided hypothesis identifies a difference between the comparison groups, although it does not identify what that difference may be (e.g., decreased or increased drug use and abuse between the two groups). The DARE program researcher who believes that drug use and abuse will decline among DARE attendees would write a one-sided hypothesis as follows: *Ninth to 12th graders who completed the DARE program during the 6th grade will show a statistically significant reduction in drug use and abuse as compared with 9th to 12th graders who did not complete the DARE program.* While it is possible and acceptable to use a one-sided hypothesis, in general, two-sided hypotheses are more commonly applied, unless there is a good justification for using a one-sided hypothesis (Farrugia et al., 2010).

Development of the research question and subsequent hypotheses is extremely important. If these are poorly developed, the researcher might use an inappropriate research design (methodology) and data collection method to complete the study. Poorly created hypotheses can also lead to unacceptable data analysis and interpretation. Farrugia et al. (2010) suggested that researchers focus their resources on considering the input of experts when choosing a topic, creating a research question, and developing hypotheses.

Types of Research Designs

An article in *Psychology Today* suggested that humans make more than 35,000 decisions every day (Krockow, 2018). It would not be surprising for a researcher to make even more decisions when doing a research project. A researcher has to decide what to study and why, who to study, what methodology to use, what data collection method to employ, and how to analyze and interpret the data, not to mention all of the ethical decisions involved in the research itself. Once a topic and research subjects are identified, one of the most important decisions is the research design. Research designs, also called methodologies, can be quantitative, qualitative, or mixed methods (Daniel, 2016). When to use each type of research design is identified in Table 4.1.

When creating a research project, the writer will typically discuss the research design in detail, being sure to provide enough details so that another researcher could replicate the study. This description will include the research design, a definition of it, identification of the advantages and

Table 4.1 When to Use Qualitative, Quantitative, and Mixed Methods Research Designs

Quantitative Methodology	Qualitative Methodology	Mixed Methods Methodology
When a deductive approach is best for the research topic	When an inductive approach is best for the research topic	When both inductive and deductive approaches will best explain the research topic
When performing experimental research	When building theory, seeking explanations or solutions	When attempting to explain contradictions in quantitative and qualitative findings from previous studies
When testing theory or universal law	When the researcher is an insider or participant in the research	When one data source may not be enough to explain the phenomenon
When using random samples	When relying on nonrandom samples	When an initial finding may need more explanation
When relying on surveys and structured questionnaires or secondary data	When field-based research is involved	When a project has multiple phases
When using statistics to explain findings	When using personal interviews or unstructured interviews to collect data	When a researcher is able to collect quantitative data first and then follow up with qualitative data to provide more detail to the quantitative findings

disadvantages of the research design, and how it relates to the study topic. The researcher will also identify any limitations the chosen design has and explain how he or she will attempt to overcome the limitations. All of this is written in a separate section of the paper called Methodology or in Chapter 3 of a master's thesis or doctoral dissertation. When writing this section of the study, the researcher will be clear and concise.

Quantitative Research

A popular research method is quantitative research. This type of research design is framed in numbers. Quantitative research is a means for testing objective theories by examining the relationship among variables, which in turn can be measured so that numbered data can be analyzed using statistical procedures (Creswell & Creswell, 2009, p. 4). Quantitative researchers often focus on deductive reasoning based in hypothesis testing and build in protections against researcher bias, alternative explanations for causal or correlational differences, and provisions for generalization and replication of the research (Creswell & Creswell, 2009). Although many approaches are used in quantitative research design, surveys or structured interviews and experimental approaches are the most universally established (Creswell & Creswell, 2009).

Quantitative research was the primary research design used in the late 19th and 20th centuries. Quantitative research has focused on true experiments in laboratories as well as quasi experiments (Creswell & Creswell, 2009). Researchers using quantitative research designs may apply experimental treatments over time or in one time period to determine any changes in behavior or beliefs. For example, a researcher may study the impact of attendance in a martial arts program on reduced aggression with peers in the classroom. Researchers may also examine the results of a nonexperimental treatment in two or more groups to determine if a cause has already occurred. Quantitative researchers examine the correlations between variables to determine if a relationship exists between them. Studying the recidivism rates among individuals who graduated from a boot camp program would be an example of a correlational design. Finally, quantitative researchers may expand their investigation into the complex relationships between variables using logistic regression, equation modeling, and other types of statistical methods (Creswell & Creswell, 2009) and may rely on longitudinal data collection to examine trends and developments (Creswell & Creswell, 2009).

Quantitative research has both advantages and disadvantages that a researcher must consider. These advantages and disadvantages are numerous, so a few are mentioned here. One of the advantages is that it is often easier and cheaper to use quantitative research when working with a large sample because surveys can be easily distributed and collected. It is easier to gather data using quantitative research because a researcher can use statistics already collected by other researchers, organizations, or agencies. For example, a source for quantitative data could be drug court completion rates and the demographics of those offenders who attended drug court. These data would already be available in the agency sponsoring the drug court, and a researcher could easily mine out the information he or she is interested in studying. Another advantage of quantitative research is that it allows a researcher to guarantee anonymity and confidentiality of respondents. This is especially useful if the researcher is studying a controversial or taboo subject.

A disadvantage of quantitative research is that it can be costly to mail surveys to many individuals and/or to purchase participants' address/email information. It can also be costly to purchase the survey software one may need to electronically collect data, such as Survey Monkey, or to analyze the data, such as IBM SPSS Statistics. A second disadvantage is that, depending on the topic being studied and the size of the participant pool, a researcher may not have the ability to generalize the findings beyond those studied. For instance, a researcher who studies marijuana use among individuals 65 years and older may not be able to generalize the findings to the entire population of individuals over age 65. Another disadvantage is the reliance on numbers to explain a phenomenon. Reducing human behavior or opinions to numbers may allow for the nuances that influence the behavior to be lost in analysis. For example, a researcher may be able to provide an account of how many police officers used deadly force in their work but may not be able to describe the officers' thought processes prior to the act.

When reading and interpreting quantitative data, the reader should consider the advantages and disadvantages as well as the data source. If the data are not collected by the researcher but are instead secondary data gathered by someone else or an agency, the data may have inherent biases and/or have been collected for some other use than the intended research project. Consider that a researcher may use data gathered by a state government to determine if youthful offenders are under the influence of drugs at the time of arrest; however, those who are marking the form may not be the police—they may be the probation officer or another court-authorized individual. This person may not have the knowledge to accurately answer the question. In this case, the data would be flawed, and anyone reading the data should be skeptical. Readers should also be careful not to overgeneralize the findings provided in a quantitative research study. Finally, when reading a quantitative study, a reader should understand how statistics work, as well as understand statistical formulas and the meanings of the statistics. Without this knowledge, numbers can be misleading, and a reader may believe that a finding means something it does not.

Qualitative Research

Researchers who are interested in why individuals do the things they do or believe the things they do may use qualitative research. Qualitative research is an "approach for exploring and understanding the meaning individuals or groups ascribe to a social or human problem" (Creswell & Creswell, 2009, p. 4). The data are typically gathered in the "subject's setting . . . and the researcher makes interpretations of the meaning of the data" (Creswell & Creswell, 2009, p. 4). A qualitative methodology allows a researcher to identify how others understand their personal experiences, determine why people engage in behaviors, and explain why certain behaviors take place (Sutton & Austin, 2015).

Qualitative research relies heavily on interviews, case studies, and ethnographies, among other methods. Researchers who use interviews ask participants about their lives and their participation in the phenomenon being studied. As an example, a researcher may interview individuals who have been victimized by crime to understand why they volunteer in victim impact panels, retelling the effect of the victimization on their lives over and over to offenders. If using a case study, a researcher may create an in-depth analysis of a case, such as a program, event, activity, or process (Creswell & Creswell, 2009). "Cases are bounded by time and activity, and researchers collect detailed information using a variety of data collection procedures over a sustained period of time" (Creswell & Creswell, 2009, p. 14; Stake, 1995; Yin, 2009, 2012, 2014). In a case study approach, a researcher may study the political focus of newspaper clippings after a major event like the terrorist attacks on the United States on September 11, 2001. Researchers may also rely on ethnographies in qualitative research. In an ethnography, a researcher "studies the shared patterns of behaviors, language, and actions of an intact cultural group in a natural setting over a prolonged period of time" (Creswell & Creswell, 2009, p. 13). This may include interviews as well as observations of the group. An example of an ethnography may be someone who studies an outlaw motorcycle gang by riding with the gang, interviewing the members, and observing them over a period of months or years. Qualitative researchers can also rely on grounded theory and phenomenological research approaches.

Qualitative research, like quantitative research, has advantages and disadvantages. Some of these benefits and limitations are discussed here. Advantages of qualitative research include its ability to explain the nuances of people's feelings and thoughts, which cannot be gained through numbers and closed-ended questions. This information can prove to be a basis for future research studies, provide new insights on a phenomenon, and/or assist in the development of survey instruments for quantitative studies (Sutton & Austin, 2015). Because qualitative research relies on a much smaller sample size than quantitative research, it can potentially save a researcher money. It may be inexpensive to keep field notes or to record interviews and listen to them later for content and analysis. However, if the researcher chooses to transcribe the interviews, it may be expensive to pay someone to assist with the process. Qualitative research allows participants to tell their story and relate their experience in their own words. By using open-ended questions that ask *why* or *how* an individual feels, thinks, or believes something, the researcher can better explain the human experience. One experience may be seen differently by two different people, and qualitative research explains the contrasts (Gaille, 2018). Finally, qualitative research allows for flexibility in data collection and analysis. As a researcher interviews a respondent, he or she can probe for more information on specific topics and develop an informal relationship that allows for conversation to flow. For example, an interview may be held while drinking coffee or within a group setting, allowing everyone to feel more comfortable.

Although there are numerous advantages to qualitative research, it also has distinct disadvantages. Qualitative research is for comparison purposes only. A researcher can compare the stories from one subject to another for similarities or differences but not for concrete, numerical measurements that can be interpreted as causation or correlation through statistical formulas (Gaille, 2018). If a researcher is not careful and does not know how to adequately interpret interview information, he or she may lose the data collected during the analysis process. To avoid this, the researcher needs to develop a clear research plan based in theory and best practices prior to collecting data. Additionally, qualitative researchers must be very careful not to incorporate their own biases into their interpretations of data. For example, although the researcher may assume that he or she knows why victims volunteer for restorative justice victim impact panels, the researcher must ignore his or her own opinion and rely solely on the information provided by the victims interviewed. Recognizing biases and assumptions ahead of time will assist in overcoming this error. Qualitative researchers should also have some experience or knowledge in the subject area so they can formulate interview questions that garner the information they really want to know about the phenomenon. The researcher should be a good interviewer so he or she knows how to ask questions, how to make the subject feel comfortable, and when to probe for additional information on topics (Gaille, 2018). If reviewing documents or making observations, the researcher should be good at spotting information related to the topic and/or taking field notes.

Qualitative research can require multiple sessions of observation and interviews (Gaille, 2018). Because questions may come up when a researcher is analyzing data that have already been collected, the researcher may need to go back to a place or subject in order to collect more data to answer the developing questions. A researcher, for example, may interview a subject but fail to ask probing questions that would have provided a richer, more descriptive picture of the subject's opinions on a topic. Because the researcher failed to follow up at the initial interview, he or she would have to request another meeting with the subject. This can consume much of the researcher's time and potentially cause a subject to withdraw from the study. The subject could become suspicious of the researcher's intentions or may just decide that it is taking up too much time to be involved in the study. Both are distinct disadvantages of qualitative research. Because qualitative research relies on a particular time, place, and person's perceptions about a phenomenon, it can be very difficult to replicate these types of studies. Finally, since qualitative research depends on the researcher's understandings and meanings applied to the data, it can lead to misleading conclusions (Gaille, 2018). In other words, when looking at the same collected information, one researcher may see a very different result than another researcher, based on each one's knowledge, past experiences, theoretical philosophy, political stance, and so on. Overcoming this bias can be extremely difficult and may make qualitative data questionable in general.

Even though many positive and negative characteristics of qualitative data were mentioned, there are other advantages and disadvantages of qualitative research. In fact, there are far too many to mention in this chapter. Nevertheless, a reader should always consider the fact that qualitative research provides rich, descriptive explanations of experiences, which numbers cannot provide. It is not generalizable to large groups, but it provides a wealth of information about human nature and perceptions of experiences. Thus, its importance in research should not be negated by any of the disadvantages mentioned.

Mixed Methods Research

Considering the pros and cons of both quantitative and qualitative research, one may wonder why one should use either approach. A researcher contemplating this would not be alone. And that is why mixed methods has gained in popularity. Creswell and Creswell (2009) explained mixed methods as a research design approach that uses both quantitative and qualitative data collection. It integrates the two types of data, philosophical assumptions, and theoretical frameworks into one research design. "The core assumption of this form of inquiry is that the integration of qualitative and quantitative data yields an additional insight beyond the information provided by either quantitative or qualitative data alone" (Creswell & Creswell, 2009, p. 5). This approach began roughly in the 1980s but has gained in popularity contemporarily. The purpose of using both research designs was to overcome the weaknesses that each individual design presented in data collection and triangulating the data sources (Jick, 1979). Although focused on patient health care models, Wisdom and Creswell (2013), described a well-designed approach to using mixed methods in studies. According to them, a mixed methods design will include the following:

1. Collecting and analyzing both quantitative (closed-ended) and qualitative (open-ended) data.

2. Using rigorous procedures in collecting and analyzing data appropriate to each method's tradition, such as ensuring the appropriate sample size for quantitative and qualitative analysis.

3. Integrating the data during data collection, analysis, or discussion.

4. Using procedures that implement qualitative and quantitative components either concurrently or sequentially, with the same sample or with different samples.

5. Framing the procedures within philosophical/theoretical models of research, such as within a social constructionist model that seeks to understand multiple perspectives on a single issue. (pp. 1–2)

To help explain a mixed methods design, consider a researcher who decides to study inmates who participate in educational programs in prison. First, the researcher may collect demographic data, information on grades and courses taken, completion rates, and other numerical data of inmates who participate in educational programs while incarcerated. The researcher may also compare the recidivism rates of inmates who participated in educational programs against those of inmates who did not participate. Next, the researcher may interview those inmates who participated in an educational program while incarcerated. The goal of the open-ended question interviews would be to understand why inmates chose to seek education while incarcerated and if they believe that their perceptions toward crime or being released and being successful in society have changed as a result of the educational program. The researcher may ask about future plans and potential re-offending during the interviews. Finally, the researcher would triangulate the data collected from both the secondary data analysis and the interviews. The researcher may find that those who successfully completed their education while incarcerated have lower re-incarceration rates. The researcher may find that a particular race has higher grades, higher participation rates, or higher completion rates. The researcher may be able to explain why this is occurring by looking for trends in the interview responses. If, for example, the researcher finds that the majority of the inmates interviewed discussed having children and being able to support their families after release as a reason for seeking education, the researcher may be able to explain the importance of familial contacts in offender treatment, reentry, recidivism, and success. Sociological or psychological theories could emerge as explanations for the findings.

When writing a mixed methods methodology study, the researcher will provide a description of the study design used—including convergent mixed methods, explanatory sequential mixed methods, exploratory sequential mixed methods, embedded designs, and multiphase designs (Creswell & Creswell, 2009; Wisdom & Creswell, 2013)—and the advantages and disadvantages of the study design. Like quantitative and qualitative research designs, the mixed methods methodology has both advantages and disadvantages. Some of the advantages are the ability to understand the contradictions often found between quantitative and qualitative data on the same topic, the ability of participants to have a voice in the findings while still allowing the researcher to ground the findings in empirical measurements, and the ability to use a multidisciplinary team of researchers and multiple research designs to explain a phenomenon (Wisdom & Creswell, 2013). Flexibility and adaptability are also advantages (Wisdom & Creswell, 2013).

Unfortunately, no research design is perfect, however. Disadvantages of using mixed methods include the fact that this approach is challenging to implement and increases the complexity of data analysis. Researchers who use mixed methods must be extremely careful in planning the design as well as in triangulating the data. Although having a multidisciplinary team is an advantage, it can also be a limitation. The researchers involved may specialize in one research design or another and can be uncomfortable with the data collection and analysis methods of the alternative design (Wisdom & Creswell, 2013). Finally, mixed methods is time-consuming and requires dedication and resources that a single researcher or even several researchers may not be able to provide (Wisdom & Creswell, 2013). Table 4.2 provides a listing of the advantages and disadvantages of each methodology discussed in this chapter.

Table 4.2 Advantages and Disadvantages of Methodologies

Quantitative Methodology	Qualitative Methodology	Mixed Methods Methodology
Advantages		
Allows for more participants in a study	Allows for greater understanding of human perception and understandings of events, circumstances, behaviors, and so on	Allows the researcher to gain both breadth and depth on a subject
Can use secondary data collected by someone else or another agency	Provides depth and detail by recording attitudes, feelings, and behaviors	Strengthens findings through triangulation
Allows for a greater chance to generalize the findings to a larger population	Can be used to build a detailed picture about individual experiences	Decreases the overreliance on statistics in trying to explain individual experiences and social understandings
Allows for greater researcher objectivity	Allows researchers to study small or unique groups of people	Allows researchers to increase their skills in data collection and interpretation
Allows for stronger reliability and validity of the data	Can provide a foundation for future research	Allows for a combination of inductive and deductive perspectives
Can more easily be replicated by other researchers	Allows a researcher to probe for more information during the interaction with the subject	
Can be more easily compared with other similar studies	More time-consuming than quantitative research	

Lessens researcher bias by allowing researchers to keep a distance from subjects	Can be expensive to have interviews transcribed and/or to travel to subjects' locations for interviews	
Researchers can guarantee anonymity and confidentiality		
Quantitative Methodology	**Qualitative Methodology**	**Mixed Methods Methodology**
Disadvantages		
Results are limited to numerical descriptions rather than detailed, grounded narrative	Fewer subjects are involved in the study, which decreases the opportunity to generalize the findings beyond the study participants	Researchers may not be skilled in both quantitative and qualitative research designs
The development of closed-ended questions can lead to structural bias and false representation of the data	Difficult to make systematic comparisons because responses from participants can be highly subjective	Using a mixed methods design may not allow for a study to be fully grounded in the theory of a discipline
Depending on the size of the sample and the topic being studied, a researcher may not be able to generalize to a larger population	Information gathered can be dependent on the interviewing skills of the researcher	It may be difficult for a researcher to explain both numbers and words when writing about the findings
	May be difficult to avoid researcher bias during the interpretation of the data	Can be time-consuming
		Consists of complex data analysis
		Challenging to implement these types of studies

As mentioned at the beginning of this section, deciding which research design is right for a project is a major task and should not be taken lightly. As Creswell and Creswell (2009) pointed out, if the problem requires an understanding of the factors that may influence an outcome, the quantitative approach is likely the best fit. If the project requires an exploration of nuances or has not been explored thoroughly in previous research, a qualitative design is probably the best approach. However, when either the quantitative or the qualitative approach alone will not help to fully understand and explain a phenomenon, the researcher will want to use a mixed methods design.

Additionally, the researcher's own personal experiences and the individuals the researcher is working with (if any) may influence the choice of research design. If a researcher is most comfortable with conversation and intimate one-on-one discussions, he or she may gravitate naturally toward a qualitative design. Those with more experience in numeric approaches or computer-based applications may feel most comfortable with a quantitative project (Creswell & Creswell, 2009). Those with time, resources, and skills in both qualitative and quantitative approaches may feel that the mixed methods approach is best for them. In addition to personal experiences, if the researcher is a student, his or her advisor or committee chair may influence the research design. The project itself can also dictate the research design. If the researcher is most interested in collecting large amounts of data, the quantitative approach should be used. Investigating a unique group or the individual perceptions of those involved in specific incidents, events, places, or behaviors works best with a qualitative design. Of course, mixed methods can be worked into any project with a carefully designed plan.

Regardless of which design is used, when writing the methodology for a study, the researcher has to clearly identify the research design, discuss why it is the most advantageous for his or her study approach, and provide a thorough discussion of the limitations of the research design. The researcher will also want to identify how he or she will overcome the limitations, if possible, or reduce their influence as much as possible on the research outcomes. After writing about the methodology, the researcher will discuss the methods used to collect the data. Table 4.3 provides a detailed list of the type of information to be included in methods sections of papers. In quantitative designs, closed-ended survey questions and experiments are often used, while in qualitative designs, researchers may use open-ended interview questions, case studies, or ethnographies. Of course, mixed methods designs use a combination of data collection instruments. In the following section, these data collection methods are discussed.

Table 4.3 Information to Include When Writing About a Methodology		
Quantitative Methodology	**Qualitative Methodology**	**Mixed Methods Methodology**
Reintroduce the topic of the study	Reintroduce the topic of the study	Reintroduce the topic of the study
Explain a quantitative methodology—what it is and the advantages and disadvantages of this type of methodology	Explain a qualitative methodology—what it is and the advantages and disadvantages of this type of methodology	Explain a quantitative methodology—what it is and the advantages and disadvantages of this type of methodology—and—explain a qualitative methodology—what it is and the advantages and disadvantages of this type of methodology
Explain the quantitative data collection method (i.e., survey, laboratory, secondary data, etc.), including a discussion of the advantages and disadvantages of the method being used	Explain the qualitative data collection method (i.e., interviews, focus groups, observation, etc.), including a discussion of the advantages and disadvantages of the method being used	Explain the quantitative and qualitative data collection methods (i.e., surveys, laboratory, interviews, observation, focus groups, etc.), including a discussion of the advantages and disadvantages of the method being used

Discuss the data collection instrument with regard to how and when it will be used, who it will be administered to, the length of participation, limitations of the instrument, the purpose of the instrument, and how it was designed	Discuss the data collection instrument with regard to how and when it will be used, who it will be administered to, the length of participation, limitations of the instrument, the purpose of the instrument, and how it was designed	Discuss all data collection instruments with regard to how and when they will be used, who they will be administered to, the length of participation for each instrument, limitations of the instruments, the purpose of the instruments, and how they were designed
Describe the unit of analysis (i.e., individuals, groups, social interactions, artifacts, etc.)	Provide concrete definitions of all terminology	Provide concrete operational definitions of all variables and terminology
Describe the limitations of the study	Describe the unit of analysis (i.e., individuals, groups, social interactions, artifacts, etc.)	Describe the unit of analysis (i.e., individuals, groups, social interactions, artifacts, etc.)
Discuss validity and reliability and explain how the researcher plans to overcome these issues	Describe the limitations of the study	Describe the limitations of the study
Provide a detailed description of the sample, including how the subjects will be identified, limitations on who will participate, issues that may arise with this sample, and how the researcher will work with the sample	Discuss validity and reliability, and explain how the researcher plans to overcome these issues	Discuss validity and reliability with regard to quantitative research and qualitative research, and explain how the researcher plans to overcome these issues
Provide a list of hypotheses, and explain how they were developed (i.e., from the literature, personal experience, past studies, etc.)	Provide a detailed description of the sample, including how the subjects will be identified, limitations on who will participate, issues that may arise with this sample, and how the researcher will work with the sample	Provide a detailed description of the samples including how they will be identified, limitations on who will participate, issues that may arise with these samples, and how the researcher will work with the samples
Discuss the possible statistical procedures to be used in analyzing the quantitative data	Provide a list of research questions, and explain how they were developed (i.e., from the literature, personal experience, past studies, etc.)	Provide a list of hypotheses and research questions, and explain how they were developed (i.e., from the literature, personal experience, past studies, etc.)
Summarize what will be presented in future paragraphs or sections of the paper, or chapters in a thesis or dissertation	Discuss the possible coding scheme to be used in analyzing the qualitative data	Discuss the possible statistical procedures to be used in analyzing the quantitative data, and explain the coding scheme to be used in analyzing the qualitative data

(Continued)

Table 4.3 (Continued)		
Quantitative Methodology	**Qualitative Methodology**	**Mixed Methods Methodology**
Provide a copy of the data collection instrument and institutional review board (IRB) information in an appendix to the paper	Summarize what will be presented in future paragraphs or sections of the paper, or chapters in a thesis or dissertation	Summarize what will be presented in future paragraphs or sections of the paper, or chapters in a thesis or dissertation
	Provide a copy of the data collection instrument and IRB information in an appendix to the paper	Provide a copy of the data collection instruments and IRB information in an appendix to the paper

Data Collection Methods/Measurement Instruments

Data collection instruments are the ways in which researchers collect data for their studies. Some of the more common data collection methods are discussed here.

Quantitative Data Collection Methods

Closed-Ended Surveys and Experiments

Quantitative methodologists use closed-ended survey questions and experiments to collect data that can be numerically analyzed for correlations and causations between the variables identified in hypotheses. In closed-ended surveys, questions and possible answers are provided to the participants, who then choose the response that most closely identifies them, their feelings, their opinions, or their behaviors. Take, for example, a closed-ended survey focused on combative behaviors in high school youths attending an alternative school. The survey may ask a youth to identify his or her grade level. A question like this may be worded as noted in Example 4.1.

Example 4.1 Sample Closed-Ended Survey Question

1. What is your grade level in school?

   a. 9th grade

   b. 10th grade

   c. 11th grade

   d. 12th grade

In this question, the participant is asked to identify his or her grade level and is provided the possible responses by the researcher. The participant then chooses the grade he or she attends in school. Notice that all possible high school grade levels are represented. The participant does not have the option of including a grade level that does not exist in a high school setting. This means that the question is mutually exhaustive, or all possible answers are provided. Additionally, because none of the grade levels are combined and no potential response allows for two grade levels to be chosen, the responses are considered mutually exclusive.

Considering the same example, a researcher who fails to provide a mutually exhaustive closed-ended survey question will face issues with lost data in coding or not being able to code the data at all. Additionally, a subject may not know which answer to choose since no one answer is correct. For example, if the responses are not mutually exclusive and a subject chooses more than one response, which should the researcher code? The researcher would not know. The sample question in Example 4.2 focuses on this issue.

Example 4.2 Sample Closed-Ended Survey Question That Is Not Mutually Exclusive

1. How many fights have you participated in at school this year?

   a. 1–2

   b. 2–4

   c. 4–6

   d. 6 or more

In this example, which answer should the respondent choose if he or she has been in four fights at school? Should the respondent choose answer (b) or answer (c)? This is not clear to the respondent. So he or she may choose both. If the respondent circles both (b) and (c), which should the researcher code? Coding answer (b) would indicate fewer fights than the respondent has actually experienced this year, while coding answer (c) would indicate more. This creates a challenge to the validity and reliability of the data.

Looking at the same question, a researcher who fails to make the closed-ended survey question mutually exhaustive could face the same challenges to validity and reliability. Consider Example 4.3 for this illustration.

The respondent who has been in more than six fights would not have an answer to choose, nor would the respondent who has not been in a fight at all. Should they just choose the highest number or lowest number provided, respectively? Is that accurate? No, they should not; and no, it is not accurate. The respondents do not have an answer that adequately indicates their behavior. If the researcher wants to use this question and these responses, he or she could add "or more" to answer (d), or provide an open-ended answer (e) that allows the participant to write in the number of fights he or

Example 4.3 Sample Closed-Ended Survey Question That Is Not Mutually Exhaustive

1. How many fights have you participated in at school this year?

   a. 1

   b. 2–3

   c. 4–5

   d. 6

she has been involved in this year at school. The researcher could also add a "0" answer choice. In conclusion, it is of dire importance that a researcher check and double-check closed-ended survey questions for exclusivity and exhaustiveness.

Another type of survey design is a Likert scale. When using a Likert scale, the researcher is likely measuring a person's attitudes or beliefs. In this type of survey design, the participant rates his or her attitude or belief on a numerical scale provided by the researcher. Typically, this scale is from 1 to 5, with 1 being the lowest ranking and 5 being the highest. In Likert scales, statements are made that allow respondents to agree or disagree with the statement. A Likert scale may appear as seen in Example 4.4.

Note that statements, not questions, are used in Example 4.4. Using questions in a Likert scale would not work since rating scales are used to determine the degree of agreement. Consider if the last question were asked in question form. It would be worded, "Do you bully others on social media?" This would typically be answered as a yes/no question. It would be very difficult for a respondent to answer by indicating an agreement rating.

Quantitative methodologists may also create experiments to measure cause and effect between two variables. This occurs more in the physical sciences, where independent variables can easily be manipulated in a laboratory, than in the social sciences, like criminal justice, where testing

Example 4.4 Sample Likert Scale Survey

Strongly Disagree	Disagree	Neither Agree nor Disagree	Agree	Strongly Agree
1	2	3	4	5

1. I feel better about myself when I post a negative comment about someone on social media.

2. I feel better about myself when I see something positive about me on social media.

3. I often use memes to explain my feelings on social media.

4. I believe that social media is used to bully others.

5. I would never bully others on social media.

Imagine you are researching a drug court in your state. Your role is to survey drug court participants on their drug involvement and behaviors. Develop 10 closed-ended questions you would use
on your survey. No more than 5 questions should focus on demographics.

in a controlled environment is nearly impossible. In an experiment, the researcher will choose a sample population to receive an independent variable (experimental group) and a sample population to receive the dependent variable (control group). The two groups will be randomly assigned but matched in characteristics as much as possible. For example, they may all be females from the same age-group, males from a correctional institution, or individuals who have the same or similar medical symptoms. The experimental group is the population who receive the new treatment, while the control group will receive either a different treatment or no treatment at all. The control group is needed to measure any differences that arise from the treatment (Center for Innovation in Research & Teaching [CIRT], n.d.). In other words, the researcher wants to know if the intervention caused changes in the experimental group. The researcher records data prior to the intervention or treatment, during the intervention or treatment, and after the intervention or treatment, if possible.

Although there are many different types of experimental designs, perhaps the most common types in the social sciences are single-shot case studies, the pre- and posttest design, and the Solomon Four Group design. In a single-shot case study, a group is provided a treatment and then posttested for changes in attitude, behavior, beliefs, and so on (CIRT, n.d.). For example, a group of juvenile offenders may attend an anger management course while on probation. Then, the offenders are posttested to see if their responses to things that anger them have changed. All single-shot case studies have disadvantages. In this example, the researcher cannot control for other variables that may have changed the subject's behaviors or beliefs, the researcher does not know the group members' knowledge of anger management techniques before attending the course, and it is very difficult for the researcher to control for validity (CIRT, n.d.).

A second common experimental design is pre- and posttesting. This can involve one group being pretested on a particular variable, provided the treatment or intervention, and then posttested on that variable (CIRT, n.d.). Another approach allows for two groups to be included in the study. Each group is randomly assigned and pretested on a particular variable. Then, the treatment or intervention is provided, and each group is posttested (CIRT, n.d.). A final approach to this design is a posttest-only group design. In this design, there are two groups, but there is no pretest. A treatment or intervention is provided to one group, and then a posttest is given to both groups to identify differences (CIRT, n.d.). Issues with the pre- and posttesting designs include the following: (a) the researcher is not able to control for variables that may affect validity, (b) other factors could influence the differences between the pre- and posttest results, (c) participants must be randomly assigned to groups and there is potential for error in random assignment, and/or (d) there may be a loss of participants between the treatment/intervention and the posttest (CIRT, n.d.).

A final experimental approach is the Solomon Four Group design. In this design, participants are randomly assigned to four groups. Two groups are pretested, and two groups are not pretested. Then, one pretested group and one group not pretested receive the treatment or intervention. Finally, all four groups are posttested to identify differences in the four groups (CIRT, n.d.). This type of design is strong because it increases the internal validity of an experimental study, especially in the social sciences. However, it still has weaknesses. It is time-consuming to plan a Solomon Four Group design. It takes a lot of resources, and several participants need to be included in the study. If working with an agency or organization, having four groups involved in a study can disrupt the schedule or workplace. The agency may not be supportive of this type of study. Pre- and posttests are usually designed as closed-ended survey questionnaires.

Formatting and Writing the Survey/Interview Questions

Following the survey design rules discussed in this section and considering how the survey will be delivered are important, whether creating a stand-alone questionnaire or a pre-/posttest to use in an experimental design. The main goal when using surveys is reliability and validity. *Reliability* refers to the consistency of the information you get, meaning that people's answers do not keep changing, and *validity* refers to the accuracy of the information, that is, its dependability (Fink & Kosecoff, 1998). If a survey is valid, it will provide the same result when measured again and again with different participants. Pilot testing a survey can assist in increasing reliability and validity. When creating a survey, a researcher should consider if the questions will be read aloud or provided to participants in writing (Harrison, 2007). If the survey is to be read aloud, the researcher will want to pretest the survey by having others read the questions or reading the questions to them and asking them if a question is clear and what it means to them (Harrison, 2007). In this way, the researcher can determine if the question makes sense when spoken and if the way the question is written is measuring what the researcher intended to measure. If the questionnaire is to be provided to participants in writing, the researcher will want to pretest the survey by having individuals complete the survey and provide feedback on the way the questions are worded, the way the responses are worded, and the format of the survey (Harrison, 2007). Researchers should consider how a survey will look when it is provided over the Internet or on paper (Harrison, 2007).

A researcher should also consider the length of a survey. Keeping a questionnaire short will encourage individuals to complete the survey. Lengthy or very wordy questionnaires may be ignored or refused by subjects (Harrison, 2007). Additionally, considering the applicability of the questions to all subjects is important. If some questions apply to part of the sample but other questions do not, the researcher may want to indicate so by saying, for example, "If you answered *no* to Question 2, skip to Question 8." In this way, subjects will move more quickly through the survey and will not provide data that are not valid or reliable to questions that do not apply to them (Harrison, 2007). Of course, the length of a survey will depend on what the researcher wants to know.

In addition to length, a researcher should consider the order of the questions on the survey. As pointed out by Harrison (2007), previous questions can affect responses to later questions. He suggested that surveys use titles to indicate various sections of the survey and provide an introduction with instructions so the respondents know what to do and why they are doing it. Fink and Kosecoff (1998) suggested that the first 10 questions in a survey relate to the topic and proceed from the subject's own behaviors to more general information. Harrison (2007) suggested that a researcher begin with general questions that are easy to answer (i.e., gender, race, occupation, etc.) and then move on to more sensitive questions (i.e., criminal behavior) toward the end of the survey. In some cases, depending on the type of demographic questions being asked and their sensitive or taboo nature (e.g., sexual preference), researchers may want to place demographic questions at the end of the survey. It has also been suggested that demographic questions are easy to answer so placing them at the end allows the subject, who may be tired if the survey is long, to answer them quickly (Fink & Kosecoff, 1998).

Additional suggestions from Harrison (2007) and others include avoiding jargon or technical terms like those used in policing or corrections, using clear and specific words that mean the same thing to everyone, and keeping responses in the ordinal level of statistics measurement. Not using double-barreled questions, which attempt to measure two variables within one question, is also a good practice (Harrison, 2007). An example of a double-barreled question would be a question worded like this: "How often do you use drugs and alcohol?" In this question, both drug use and alcohol use are being measured, but it is unclear which of the variables the respondent is replying to, especially if the person uses drugs but not alcohol or vice versa. Finally, a researcher will want to avoid asking leading questions (Harrison, 2007). For example, the researcher would not want to ask, "Do you believe the federal government should end the focus on the failed war on drugs?" By identifying the war on drugs as a failure, the researcher is potentially biasing the participant's response. In other words, the respondent could interpret the question as the researcher wanting him or her to answer "yes."

While there are many other survey rules that are covered in a research methods course, the final issue mentioned here is format. A researcher should design a survey to be aesthetically pleasing. A questionnaire's appearance is important (Fink & Kosecoff, 1998). If a respondent is taking the survey by himself or herself, confusion can occur if the survey is not designed in a clear format. Survey questions should be numbered and have clearly marked answers that require a participant to circle the response. Enough space should be provided to allow respondents to write in answers if there are open-ended response opportunities (Fink & Kosecoff, 1998). Furthermore, the researcher may want to number pages if the survey has multiple pages; and if using branched questions (questions that allow respondents to skip ahead), the researcher will want to make sure the skipping instructions are clearly stated. Computer-assisted surveys are sometimes the simplest format to use when allowing for branched questions because the computer can skip to the next relevant question depending on the answer provided by the respondent (Fink & Kosecoff, 1998).

Qualitative Data Collection Methods

Interviews

Although qualitative methodologists may not rely on survey data, they do use interviews in data collection. In an interview, the researcher will ask both general and specific open-ended questions to explore or investigate a phenomenon. To do this, the researcher will rely on an interview schedule or an open-ended survey design. In an interview schedule, the researcher uses *how* and *why* questions, which ask the participant to explain, rather than predetermined responses, which force the individual to choose an answer. Example 4.5 demonstrates questions used in an interview schedule.

Example 4.5 Sample Interview Schedule Questions

1. How did you find out about the restorative justice program in Martin County?

2. What were you told about the program and your possible role in the program when you decided to volunteer?

3. How did you decide what to say during your presentation describing what happened to you during the criminal incident?

4. If given the opportunity, what would you change about the program provided by Martin County?

The researcher uses the interview schedule to guide the interview so that he or she includes all of the variables being investigated in the study. The researcher, however, will also ask probing questions as the participant talks. So, for example, in response to Question 4 of the sample interview schedule in Example 4.5, if the person says that she would change the types of offenders attending the program, the researcher may ask, "What type of offenders do you think would best benefit from the program? Why? Have you mentioned this to the program coordinator? What did he say?" Every participant may not have suggested changes to the program in Martin County, so the probing questions are not necessary; or the interviewees may provide the information in their initial response, making the probing questions redundant. Thus, the probing questions may not be included in every interview.

Open-Ended Surveys

Qualitative methodologists may also rely on open-ended question surveys. In this design, as noted in Example 4.6 on youth fighting at school, the researcher asks a question and allows the respondent to provide a written or verbal response. These types of questions provide participants the ability to describe their behaviors, opinions, or feelings in their own words.

Example 4.6 Sample Open-Ended Question Survey

1. How many fist fights have you had at school this year?

2. Thinking of the last three fist fights you had at school, explain what caused them.

3. How did the school respond to the fist fights?

4. How did your parents (or guardian) respond to the fighting at school?

Using interviews and open-ended survey questionnaires has certain disadvantages. One disadvantage is that the coding process is more complicated. Instead of coding predetermined responses into numbers, the researcher has to analyze the written or verbal words for themes. Then, the researcher has to develop categories that identify responses with similarities and responses with gross differences from all the other interviews. The categories may be grounded in the literature and past research or based on experiences with similar programs. The goal is keeping the categories and themes as precise as possible and avoiding researcher bias (Fink & Kosecoff, 1998). In many cases, these types of measurements require an elaborate coding system (Fink & Kosecoff, 1998). As a result, qualitative measurement instruments face reliability and validity issues not found in quantitative approaches.

Even with the disadvantages, qualitative measurements have many advantages, especially when investigating why people believe the way they do (Fink & Kosecoff, 1998). If a researcher develops ways to deal with validity and reliability concerns (e.g., the use of precise coding systems), the researcher can provide the field with rich, detailed descriptive data, which cannot be obtained through numbers. Investigating unique or distinctive groups that may have exclusive membership or may be difficult to access in large numbers is another advantage of qualitative instruments. For example, a researcher may not be able to gain access to all members of a nudist colony to investigate why they participate in this type of perceived deviant behavior but might be able to get a few members to agree to individual interviews or a small focus group. The other advantages of qualitative methodologies discussed in this chapter also apply to interviews and open-ended surveys.

Other Qualitative Measurements

Other qualitative measurement instruments include field notes taken during observation studies and content analysis. Although this chapter will not spend a lot of time on these two concepts, they should at least be briefly discussed. A researcher may engage in observation of individuals and/or a phenomenon. In this case, the individuals and their activities will not be interrupted. When a researcher uses observation studies, he or she will document the setting and provide descriptions of the participants and what he or she observes. It is important that the researcher use thorough field notes so that the information can be turned into data and conclusions. As with interviews, a well-defined coding system must be identified prior to the observations. Additionally, because of the distance between the researcher and those being observed, the researcher has to consider the potential for error in the interpretation of the observations. In other words, what the researcher thinks he or she has observed may be viewed differently by another observer. Overcoming the potential validity and reliability issues apparent in observation can be a challenge.

A content analysis is another form of qualitative research. In a content analysis, a researcher uses documents to explore a phenomenon. The researcher gathers a number of documents and uses a sample of them to develop a coding scheme. Then, the researcher identifies a panel and trains them in the coding scheme to make sure that what the researcher has defined as variables will be identified and defined the same way by the panel members. Finally, once the coding scheme is established, the researcher analyzes all of the documents using the coding scheme. When writing the research methods section of the paper, the researcher will provide detailed information on the coding scheme and process, in addition to a thorough discussion of how the coding scheme was confirmed. Suffice it to say that as qualitative research the methodological disadvantages identified above apply to these approaches, and researchers must be mindful in their design, process, and analysis.

Mixed Methods Data Collection

Since the mixed methods approach includes the data measurement instruments used in quantitative and qualitative methodologies, there is no need to discuss them again here. To better understand this approach, consider the following examples. A researcher studying citizen perception of the police in a high-crime area may use a survey with closed- and open-ended questions, allowing for both types of data analysis. Another researcher may analyze newspaper reporting on a police-involved shooting in an urban area and then interview those involved. As noted previously, a mixed methods approach combines multiple types of data measurements and consists of complex data analysis procedures, as well as other issues. A researcher who employs mixed methods will be required to discuss both quantitative and qualitative processes and procedures in the methods section of a paper and the advantages and limitations of each in the study.

When cooking, a chef will follow specific steps to create a dish. For example, the chef may wait to put the rice in the dish last so that it does not overcook and become hard or mushy. The chef may begin by preparing a pan with butter or oil so that the meat does not stick to the pan. If the chef decides to share the dish with others so they too can cook it, he will likely provide these details so that others can cook the same dish with the same results at a later time. The methods section is like a recipe. It has to include the details of the study from beginning to end so that another researcher, at another time, can replicate the study with the same or similar results. When writing the methods section of a paper, the researcher will include a detailed discussion of the data measurement instrument and when and how the instrument will be provided to participants. "This includes procedures for administering measurement instruments, details of implementation for any intervention (e.g., length of treatment, time of day) and difference of conditions in treatment group (if there were multiple groups)" (Bui, 2014, pp. 151–152). Detailed descriptions of the procedures are extremely important in this section for replicability by other researchers and the credibility of the study (Bui, 2014). Again, reviewing Table 4.3 will help identify what should be included when writing the methods section of a paper.

Consider an experimental quantitative study, for example. A researcher can divide the description into three categories: pretest, treatment/intervention, and posttest. Then, the researcher can describe the steps in each process so that it is clear to the reader how the study proceeded (Bui, 2014). If using a survey, the researcher can do the same by describing the survey, any instructions provided to the respondents, how the survey will be given (i.e., written or verbal), how the survey will be collected when completed, and how the results will be stored and analyzed. In qualitative observation studies, as another example, a researcher will describe the conditions in which the observations were conducted, including the time, place, weather, frequency, and so on, and the role the observer played in the observation—participant/participant-observer (Bui, 2014). The researcher will also explain how field notes were taken and what was included in the notes. Although the survey or measurement instrument description is provided in the methods section, a copy of the data collection tool is included as an appendix so readers can see the questions for themselves. The coding scheme is explained in the methods section.

Regardless of the measurement techniques used in a study, the researcher must eventually make sense of the information collected. This process is called data analysis. Knowing how to write the findings and providing enough details on the level of measurement are important. Data analysis and the information included in a research methods section are discussed next.

Data Analysis

Just as there are many ways to collect data, there are also many ways to analyze data (Bui, 2014). Which statistical procedures are used depends on the design of the study. If a study has a descriptive design, the researcher may only report descriptive statistics. If the study is a comparison between groups—experimental/pretest/posttest—the researcher will use tests of significance or inferential statistics. If the study is explanatory and makes predictions, the researcher will use tests of association, which are included in inferential statistics (Hazlett, n.d.). Even though the data are not actually analyzed and findings are not reported in the research methods section of a paper, the template for how the data will be analyzed is described here. In the research methods section of a paper or thesis, the researcher provides the reader with a description of how the data will be collected, what levels of measurement will be used, and how the data will be analyzed.

Quantitative Data

In this section of a quantitative paper, the researcher will identify the variables being measured in table form. Table 4.4 demonstrates how this will look to the reader. By doing this, the researcher is able to provide a clear indication of what variables are being measured, how, and the level of measurement for each variable. The researcher is also able to clarify for the reader the independent, dependent, and control variables, if any. Finally, this process assists in coding for later data analysis. By identifying the level of measurement and the coding scheme, the researcher is one step closer to data analysis.

Table 4.4 Table for Variables

Variable Name	Label and Values	Level of Measurement
Satisfaction—dependent variable	Job satisfaction of sworn officers 1 = *strongly disagree* 2 = *disagree* 3 = *neutral* 4 = *agree* 5 = *strongly agree*	Ordinal (ranked from high to low)
Gender—independent variable	Sex 0 = female 1 = male	Nominal (categories that cannot be ranked)
Service	Years of police service with department Open-ended question	Interval (actual number of years)

As identified in Table 4.4, the level of measurement determines the type of statistical procedures used to appropriately assess the variable and any relationships it has to other variables. Descriptive statistics focus primarily on scores as a group. These can include all levels of measurement—nominal, ordinal, interval, ratio—and rely primarily on measures of central tendency—mean, median, mode—and variability—range and standard deviation—to describe the data (Theobald, n.d.). As an example of descriptive data, a researcher may include the number of male police officers who participated in the job satisfaction survey categorized in Table 4.4 or the number of officers who have worked at the police department for less than 5 years and indicated that they strongly agreed that they are satisfied with their jobs. Descriptive statistics can measure a relationship between two variables and provide the degree of relationship or association between the two variables (Theobald, n.d.).

A quantitative study may also use inferential statistics to test the hypotheses. In these types of statistical formulas, a significance level is determined between two or more variables. The null hypothesis is tested and either found to be supported by the data or not. When using inferential statistics, a researcher may employ *t* tests, tests for analysis of variance, chi-square formulas, multiple regression, and other statistical formulas.

For this section of a paper, the researcher should provide a comprehensive explanation of the level of measurement, the type of statistical approach that is appropriate (descriptive or inferential), which variables will be compared or correlated, and which statistical formulas will be used. Although the results of the data are not reported in the methods section, the writer will provide the recipe for how the data will be analyzed.

Qualitative Data

In a qualitative study, numbers and statistical formulas may have little purpose. A researcher may use descriptive statistics to describe the sample, such as race, gender, religion, type of victimization, and so on, but will not

Mapping Becomes a Powerful Tool for Police Departments

By Laura Nightengale of the Journal Star

Agencies track, evaluate, analyze, and share data collected by officers to operate more efficiently. The goal is to take the massive amounts of crime data and craft easy-to-understand snapshots of criminal and police activity. The technology provides officers an added tool to pinpoint hotbeds for crime and suspects. When investigating a string of car burglaries, for instance, police know that suspects tend to stay close to home or develop a routine. By tracking that information, police can try to nab a suspect, and by sharing it with the public, they can warn potential victims to lock up and look out. Prior to crime mapping technology, police had to work harder to identify trends in crime and to get that information out to the public.

necessarily be able to describe the respondent's words in numerical form. Since qualitative studies are mostly narrative, the data analysis involves coding through categorization (Bui, 2014). In this approach, the researcher will label and group the data into meaningful themes. One can think of coding in qualitative studies as similar to doing laundry. When washing clothes, a person will sort the laundry into whites, colors, blue jeans, towels, and so forth. Or the launder may sort by water type (i.e., hot or cold wash requirements) (Bui, 2014). How the sorting of information will be done has to be described in the methods section. Instead of conducting tests of significance or correlation, qualitative researchers may keep reflective journals about their observations and thoughts, write memos to themselves, or audio record their thoughts (Bui, 2014). These approaches are described in the methods section along with the coding scheme created prior to commencing the study and/or the coding process if using open, axial, and selective coding. If a transcriber or computer software is going to assist in the data analysis, it is also mentioned here.

Other Information Included in the Methods Section

As one has likely noted, the methods section is a critical portion of any research paper (Bui, 2014). It provides thorough details on the study's design and builds credibility for the study. It also allows others to replicate the study's design and statistical analysis. Even though this chapter has provided a lot of information so far, there is still more material a researcher will include in this section of a paper. This includes operational definitions of the terminology used in the hypothesis or study, the setting and time frame of the study, a description of the participants, the intervention or treatment, IRB information, and the limitations of the study. These segments will be discussed briefly here.

Operational Definitions

Operational definitions define the terminology used in the study and in the hypotheses. Operational definitions are usually short paragraphs that state how the literature has defined the term and how the researcher will concretely define or measure the concept (Hazlett, n.d.). Think about social class as an example. Often students want to label social class as upper, middle, and lower; however, these terms are not operational or measurable because what may be considered middle class by one person may not be middle class to another. In an operational definition, the researcher provides a meaning that is shared by all and makes sense to all. So, using the social class example, a researcher may define the middle class as individuals making $55,000 to $80,000 per year. Operational definitions not only help the reader and the participants in understanding the terms, but they can also assist when identifying issues in validity and reliability.

The Setting and Time Frame

The researcher should identify the research site and explain how the data will be collected at the site. If, for example, a researcher is surveying elementary school students, the researcher will describe the school and in what classrooms the survey is provided to participants. In general, the setting is described in broad terms (e.g., an elementary school in Central Florida) and then in more specific terms (e.g., fifth-grade English classrooms were used to distribute the survey) (Bui, 2014). Once the setting has been established, the discussion should include a time frame. If a one-time survey was provided, the researcher will mention the month when it was provided. Using the school example, a researcher may say that the survey was distributed to students in April 2019. If the study involves a longitudinal design or a specific period of time because of a historical event, the researcher will indicate this as well. The setting and time frame are usually described in a paragraph or two, with enough details to enable the reader to understand and, if required, repeat the process.

Exercise 4.6

Suppose you are writing a methods section for a research study on public intoxication. Identify the setting you would use to observe this type of behavior and the time frame you would employ.

The Participants

In this portion of the methods section, the researcher explains the sampling plan used to select participants for the study and describes the individuals who participated in the study. The sampling plan can include a random sample or a nonrandom sampling design (Bui, 2014). The researcher explains why the specific sampling plan that was used was the most advantageous for the study and how the sample was chosen from the larger population. The researcher will also describe how long the participants were involved in the study. If it was a one-time survey completed in 15 minutes, the researcher will state that to the reader. Finally, the researcher includes a full and thorough description of the individuals who participated in the study, along with any exclusion and inclusion criteria used in choosing the participants. The researcher also includes a statement of generalizability. If the findings cannot be generalized beyond the participants included in the study, the researcher will make this clear to the reader (Bui, 2014).

The Intervention or Treatment

The researcher uses this section to describe the intervention or treatment administered in the course of the study or prior to the study. A full description of how and when the intervention or treatment was given and the materials used to administer the intervention or treatment is provided. The researcher will likely discuss how data will be protected once collected, and if there is a likelihood of any issues or concerns during the treatment or intervention, they are discussed here. Ethical issues are also identified in this segment of the methods section.

IRB Information

If the researcher performed or will perform a study using human participants, the researcher will need IRB approval. This approval is obtained prior to any data collection, and it is during the study design process that most researchers complete the IRB approval forms and respond to any issues or concerns the IRB board may have about the study. The IRB process can actually assist a researcher in designing the study because the forms ask about variables, definitions, sampling design, data collection instruments, and ethical issues. The researcher will disclose any information about the IRB approval in this section (application has been made to the IRB, approval has been granted, etc.), and a copy of the IRB approval will be provided in the appendix section of the paper.

Limitations of the Study

Since no methodology is absolute, no survey or interview is flawless, and all statistical procedures have strengths and weaknesses, there will never be a perfect study (Hazlett, n.d.). The end of the methods section usually provides a summary of the limitations of the study design, data collection methods, and statistical procedures used. In this section, the researcher will identify the questions this study will not address and how the researcher will attempt (or has attempted) to overcome as many of the limitations as possible.

Figure 4.1 briefly lists the components of a methods section. A more detailed explanation of the components is found in Table 4.3. The actual format of the methods section will depend on what is being studied and what the researcher is attempting to find out. Not all items may apply to every study. The researcher will need to decide what is applicable to his or her study and what is not.

Figure 4.1 Information to Be Included in a Methods Section

- A description of the research methodology or approach

- The research design, including the independent, dependent, and control variables, operational definitions, and hypotheses or research questions

- A description of the intervention or treatment

- Pilot studies, if applicable

- Sampling procedures

- Data collection instruments, including survey description, scales, questionnaires, experiment design, observation plans

- IRB information

- Data collection process and statistical analysis, including the coding scheme or the list of variables and levels of measurements

- Limitations and weaknesses of the methodology, data collection instrument, and statistical procedures

CHAPTER SUMMARY

The methods section of a paper is critical in explaining to the reader how the study will be or was completed. The researcher provides a wealth of information in this section, including the items listed in Figure 4.1. It is the methods section that provides the recipe for replication of the study. It also supports the credibility of the study by demonstrating that the researcher followed standard scientific rules and guidelines in completing the study (Bui, 2014). Furthermore, the methods section provides the groundwork for accurate data analysis and interpretation (Bui, 2014).

QUESTIONS FOR CONSIDERATION

1. In your opinion, why is it so difficult to narrow a topic for a research study?

2. Identify at least two advantages and disadvantages of quantitative, qualitative, and mixed methods approaches.

3. Write one null hypothesis and one alternative hypothesis for a study involving alcohol binge drinking among college sophomores.

4. If your college professor asked you to create a study involving a survey, what type of study would you suggest and why?

5. What is the difference between descriptive statistics and inferential statistics?

CHAPTER 5

Writing Research and Grant Proposals

Criminal justice students and researchers will often find it necessary to write proposals. The most common research proposal assignments for criminal justice students and researchers include research, conference, and grant proposals. Professors will sometimes ask students to write a proposal detailing the student's plans for a research project, and it is often the first step for a doctoral student to obtain permission to write a dissertation (University of Southern California Libraries, 2019). Students, researchers, and scholars often submit proposals for conference presentations. Similarly, grant proposal writers who seek to obtain funding from the federal government, private organizations, and philanthropists must also complete a proposal that describes the project in detail and lists how the grant money will be spent. A proposal is used to justify the need for a project and outlines the potential costs of the project (University of Southern California Libraries, 2019). This chapter introduces students to several types of abstracts and proposals. Sample proposals are included.

A proposal is a detailed document that describes a research idea or a problem and outlines how the issue can be studied or addressed. A research proposal justifies the need to study a problem and proposes the way in which the research should be conducted (University of Southern California Libraries, 2019). Students and criminal justice professionals may want to share their studies at a professional conference. A conference proposal tells the reader about the project, why it's appropriate for presentation at the particular conference, and the writer's qualifications. A grant proposal is similar to a research proposal, but this proposal requests funding to complete a study or pay for a project to address the problem. A book proposal requires great detail and knowledge of the subject matter. Book proposals are quite lengthy since publishers often want to see an outline of the proposed chapters, sample chapters, and a timeline for completing the book.

Writing a Research Proposal

When a student's research project is more complex than simply gathering information from secondary sources, professors will often ask the student to write a research proposal. The research proposal is a detailed plan of the project, written so that a professor or reviewer can approve the project. Auri-acombe (2005) defines the research project as

> a key document . . . that . . . looks both back and forward that provides the reader with a clear and consistent outline of what topic is to be studied, what the objectives of the research are, what type of study will be conducted (the research design), how the research will be conducted (the research methodology), as well as the envisaged time frame and resources required. (p. 379)

These types of projects often involve gathering primary data or studying human participants. Primary sources include research, publications, reports, interviews, and other original material (Schiffhorst & Schell, 1991). Secondary sources are created with the support of primary sources. Primary sources give a truer sense of the topic than any secondary source could provide (Bombaro, 2012). The study is said to involve human participants whenever people are observed, interviewed, surveyed, or asked to complete tasks associated with the study. A sample research proposal can be found in Example 5.1.

Note: secondary sources will always be supported by a primary source.

Students and researchers should be familiar with citation and reference guidelines and should make every effort to avoid plagiarism. Plagiarism is defined as using another person's thoughts, ideas, or words as one's own or failing to properly identify the source of the information. One study suggests that "almost 40% of the proposals submitted by graduate students contained notable plagiarism, including copying and pasting of text from websites, failure to paraphrase, and failure to put quotation marks around direct quotes" (Gilmore, Strickland, Timmerman, Maher, & Feldon, 2010).

plagiarism = simply don't do it!

A professor or organization requesting a research proposal may specify the organization of a report; the following section offers a general format for arranging a research proposal.

Elements of a Research Proposal

Purpose/Significance of the Study

A problem statement or study objective is clearly stated within the first paragraph of a research proposal. Much like a thesis statement for an essay, the problem statement tells the reader the purpose of the study, if it has practical significance, and whether it contributes to the current literature (Babbie, 2001).

Literature Review

what a literature review actually is

The literature review examines in detail studies that have been previously completed that are closely associated with the research topic. The literature is reviewed to determine what others have said about the topic, what theory applies to the topic, and what research has been done previously (Babbie, 2001). The writer should also include a discussion of each study's relevance to the research project, any methodological errors (if appropriate), and how the current study can address those errors.

Subjects for the Study

This section describes who or what will be analyzed to collect data. The section particularly applies to human participants. The researcher should explain who the study participants are, how they will be located, if the research will affect them in any way, and what the researcher will do to protect them from harm (Babbie, 2001). All projects involving human participants must obtain approval from the institution's institutional review board prior to beginning the study.

Research Design

In this section, the researcher identifies the research design as quantitative (e.g., exploratory, descriptive, experimental) or qualitative (e.g., observational, cohort, longitudinal). The dependent and independent variables are defined, as are the hypotheses to be tested. According to Babbie (2001), this section should include the population, sampling frame, sampling method, sample size, data collection method, completion rate, and methods of analysis.

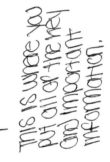

This is where you put all of the key and important information.

Data Collection

Here, the researcher describes how the data to be tested will be collected. Primary data can be collected by conducting an experiment, completing a survey, or direct observation of the study participants. Criminal justice data on a variety of topics can also be obtained from the Bureau of Justice statistics (https://www.bjs.gov/index.cfm?ty=dctp), the FBI Uniform Crime Reporting System (https://www.fbi.gov/services/cjis/ucr), and the National Archive of Criminal Justice Data (https://www.icpsr.umich.edu/icpsrweb/NACJD/discover-data.jsp).

Treatment of the Data

This section describes how the data will be analyzed. If the study is quantitative, what statistical methods (e.g., t test, analysis of variance, regression) will be used? If the study is qualitative, what identifying trends or patterns in the study subject are the primary focus of the research project? The author should discuss trends or patterns in the study by identifying common statements, opinions, or beliefs. The author should also identify outliers or uncommon findings, as is done with the statistics in a quantitative paper.

Sample Research Proposal

The following sample includes the major sections of a research proposal. Please note that this sample is meant to be informative and has been edited to save space. It is not meant to represent a complete proposal that a student or criminal justice professional might submit for review. This sample essay includes reference citations within the text, but a full references section is not included as part of the sample,

Sample on the next page is brief explanation.

Example 5.1 Sample Research Proposal

Introduction

The extant literature is replete with examples of how civil litigation is affecting the police, their operational policies and practices. Rarely a day goes by when the national headlines do not carry a leading story of an officer or agency of the law being sued for using excessive force or violating someone's constitutional rights. Civil litigation filed against police agencies is not a new phenomenon; however the frequency with which these suits are now being filed is. Now more than at any other time in our history, police actors and agencies are being forced to take steps to shield themselves from civil litigation (Bell, 2001; Christensen, 2001; Fisk, 2001). Little research exists examining how this management decision affects the quantity or quality of lawsuits filed against any individual police agency. More to the point, no literature exists or study has been conducted within the state of Florida examining this issue specifically.

Purpose of the Study

The purpose of the study is to determine if these accreditation boards make a difference in decreasing the number of lawsuits filed against accredited agencies. Similarly, this research will also examine if law enforcement accreditation serves to limit or reduce the overall burden placed on taxpayers in the financial judgments handed down where the police are found to be at fault for violating the civil liberties of their constituents.

Each of these research inquiries is an open empirical question, and none have been empirically tested in any sound methodological manner. While there is anecdotal evidence supplied by CALEA regarding the financial benefit for agencies licensing with them, these studies have not been soundly empirically tested. If it can be empirically proven that accreditation does lessen the liability of sovereign police entities, more police organizations should be willing to pay the cost in time and capital to become fully accredited.

Significance of the Study

Although accreditation was established and implemented in law enforcement 25 years ago by CALEA, very little empirical research has been completed in the field. Almost no sound methodological studies have been conducted attesting to the cost savings of individual agencies that undergo the rigorous review brought about through these processes. At the state level, the literature is completely silent.

At the present time, there is very little literature in the professional or practitioner arena attesting to the benefit to law enforcement agencies undergoing this review process. Further, the extant literature remains silent on the issue as to whether CFA accreditation reduces the lawsuits filed against participating law enforcement agencies. Hence, if a study could establish a relationship between accredited status and reduced frequency and/or severity of lawsuits, it seems reasonable that prudent law enforcement executives could more easily justify participating in this costly, voluntary process.

Theory

Linking the process of law enforcement accreditation to a theoretical body of literature is a tenuous task and one that is not easily made. However, there is a significant body of literature in the management sciences that details how professional bodies that control and police their own rank and file are generally viewed and held in higher regard. Further membership in these organizations (i.e., professionally licensed agencies) is paramount to their continuing survival as an organizational unit. With this literature in mind, it is possible to link the accreditation process with the literature on professional organizations.

Hypotheses

1. H_0: There is no statistically significant difference in the number of lawsuits suffered by accredited Florida law enforcement agencies and nonaccredited Florida agencies.

   H_a: Accredited Florida law enforcement agencies suffer fewer lawsuits than nonaccredited Florida law enforcement agencies.

2. H_0: There is no statistically significant difference in the severity of court-ordered judgments suffered by accredited Florida law enforcement agencies and nonaccredited Florida agencies.

   H_a: Court-ordered judgments paid by accredited Florida law enforcement agencies are less than those paid by nonaccredited Florida agencies.

Literature Review

This section describes research that has been done previously. The writer should also include a discussion of each study's relevance to the research project, any methodological errors (if appropriate), and how the current study can address those errors.

   Christensen (2001) writes that Miami has paid more than $19 million in civil liability claims to constituents since 1990 to resolve more than 110 federal and state lawsuits for actions by its officers. This figure however represents a conservative estimate since another 70 lawsuits are pending. Less quantifiable costs of lawsuits include salaries for legal staff, legal fees paid to outside lawyers, and various other costs such as court reporter and copying charges. The lawsuits fall into five general categories: false arrest, excessive force, shootings, wrongful death, and federal civil rights violations. The city has responded by changing procedures to improve documentation of events and increasing training for officers. This study

supports the theory that lawsuits against law enforcement agencies are growing.

Methodology

This section describes the population, research design, instrument, manner of data collection, and treatment of the data.

Research Design

The research design is quasi-experimental. Dependent and independent variables are clearly identified. The central independent variable is accreditation, and the dependent variables include total lawsuits filed against the agency, total amount (dollars) of court-ordered judgments paid by the agency, and total amount (dollars) of out-of-court settlements paid by the agency. Hypotheses have been formulated, and parametric statistical analyses will be conducted on the data to test the hypotheses.

Specific Procedures

The following procedures will be followed to complete the study:

1. Institutional review board application and approval

2. Designing the survey instrument

3. Pretesting the instrument

   a. Focus group

   b. Final check

4. Pilot study

   a. Mailing the survey instrument to 10 accredited and 10 nonaccredited agencies

   b. Collecting and analyzing the data

   c. Evaluating the instrument and making necessary changes

5. Mailing the survey instrument

6. Collecting data

7. Analyzing the data

8. Completing the study

(Continued)

(Continued)

Description of the Population

This study is limited to the 100 accredited law enforcement agencies in the state of Florida and an equal number of nonaccredited Florida law enforcement agencies. The population represents about 52% of the total number of law enforcement agencies in the state. As such, the findings of this study can be generalized to the population of law enforcement agencies within the state of Florida.

Description of the Instrument

The instrument includes a cover page, an instruction page, and four sections of questions —asking a total of 18 questions. The survey instrument for the experimental group will be mailed to the agency's accreditation manager. A copy of the survey instrument is included as an addendum to this document.

Pilot Study

A pilot study of the survey instrument will be conducted to ensure the instrument's reliability and validity. The pilot instrument will be designed based on the literature review and an analysis of the survey instruments used by other researchers in the field of study.

Data Collection

Following the pilot study, the data for this research project will be collected by a survey instrument sent to the 100 accredited law enforcement agencies in the state of Florida and an equal number of Florida nonaccredited agencies. The survey packet will be mailed to the agency's accreditation manager since this person is responsible for and has the most current information about the accreditation process. Surveys mailed to the 100 nonaccredited agencies will be sent to the chief or

SOURCE: Author created.

sheriff, informing him or her of the nature of the study. All packets will include an assurance of confidentiality.

Treatment of the Data

Data will be analyzed using ordinary least squares statistical methods such as *t* test, ANOVA, and regression where appropriate.

Limitations of the Study

This researcher acknowledges the work of Langworthy and Travis (1998), which suggests the inclusion of large agencies may introduce unacceptable levels of bias. But of the 106 Florida law enforcement agencies accredited by CALEA, CFA, or both, just 54% (N = 57) employ less than 100 officers. As such, about one half of the sampling frame is lost by not including agencies with more than 100 employees. Rather than eliminating a significant portion of the sample, then, we will avoid the "big city" bias, which has to date confounded many research studies, by including all accredited agencies in the analysis while controlling for agency size.

Conclusion

The purpose of this study is to determine if a causal relationship exists between accreditation and the frequency and severity of liability claims for Florida's accredited law enforcement agencies. Using a quasi-experimental design, the researcher will collect data from 200 Florida law enforcement agencies through the use of a survey instrument. The instrument has been pretested to ensure its reliability and validity. The data will be analyzed using appropriate OLS methods.

Bibliography

This section would contain the works cited in the research proposal.

Writing a Conference Proposal

Students, professors, and criminal justice professionals often attend academic and professional conferences to learn about the work of others, share their own work, and network with others in their discipline and profession. Before a paper can be submitted for presentation at a conference, the presenter is required to submit a conference proposal.

Conference proposals are most often submitted by email, so the writer should follow proper email etiquette. Emails should be written in a formal tone. The content of the email should be free from grammar errors and should be left justified. There should be limited use of slang or jargon, and no emojis.

The layout of a formal email is similar to that of an official letter with the exception of the header. Unlike a letter, a prescribed header is not necessary. Instead of providing an official header with the sender's name, title, and address at the top of the email, the sender can place this information below the signature line. Additionally, a recognized day, time, or year does not need to be placed at the top of an email. Since an email system, like Yahoo, Google mail, or some other business software system, will generally include the sender's name, recipient's name, email addresses of both, and date in the email sending system, the writer does not need to provide this information in a formal way at the top of the body of the email. Instead, the email can just begin with the salutation and body paragraph. The topic of the email should be included in the subject line of the email.

Conference proposals are generally quite short—typically just a paragraph or two written in the format of an abstract. The proposal should include the title of the paper, presentation, or poster board and the names of the primary and secondary authors. A brief summary of the study should be provided in one or two sentences. The sample, data, data treatment, and findings should be described in enough detail so that readers have an adequate understanding of the purpose of the study and how it was conducted. Finally, list any data, charts, graphs, or other materials that will be included in the presentation or shared with the audience. A sample conference proposal can be found in Example 5.2.

Sample Conference Proposal

The following sample includes the major sections of a conference proposal. Please note that this sample is meant to be informative and has been edited to save space. It is not meant to represent a complete proposal that a student or criminal justice professional might submit for review.

Example 5.2 Sample Conference Proposal

Picking Good Apples: Organizational Determinants of Crimes Committed by Law Enforcement Officers

Steven Hougland, PhD, Florida Sheriffs Association

Coauthor 1: Jennifer Allen, PhD, Nova Southeastern University

Coauthor 2: Tae M. Choo, PhD, University of North Georgia

Abstract

This study seeks to identify organizational characteristics in Florida police agencies where officers have committed criminal acts. In order to conduct the analysis, two data sets are used. The first includes 12,272 records for criminal acts committed by officers from 321 county and municipal law enforcement agencies in Florida, and the second identifies organizational characteristics of Florida police agencies. The objectives of this study are important for several reasons: Identifying organizational correlates to crime committed by officers could inform policymakers on the efficacy of commonly accepted administrative controls in policing, and identifying these organizational characteristics will inform scholarship on police organization best practices. The authors will present the study data and analysis findings. Policy implications will be discussed.

SOURCE: Author created.

Writing a Grant Proposal

As noted above, when the term *proposal* is used in academia, it can mean a few things. First, it can mean research writing where a student or someone else presents a study idea, including the study design, sample, data collection instrument, and analysis, to a conference, an evaluator, or another group of academics. Second, it can mean that someone has an idea for a grant and decides to submit the paperwork for review to a funding agency. Many times, funding agencies themselves send out requests for proposals that specify what they are funding, deadlines to make requests, and details of what should be included in the grant funding request. One of the top grant funders is the U.S. federal government, although states, local municipalities, private companies and groups, individuals, and foundations also fund grant ideas.

> A grant is a way the government funds your ideas and projects to provide public services and stimulate the economy. Grants support critical recovery initiatives, innovative research, and many other programs listed in the Catalog of Federal Domestic Assistance (CFDA). (Grants.gov, n.d.-a)

To request a grant, a grant proposal or application must be submitted. A grant proposal is like a research proposal, but a grant proposal requests funding to complete a study or pay for a project to address a specific problem. For example, a police department may want to purchase body cameras, study elderly victims of credit card fraud, or start a youth program to deter crime. However, the police department may not have the funds in their general budget to complete these projects. Instead, the police department can reach out to local agencies or groups for funding, such as the Kiwanis or a local corporation, or they can investigate potential funding opportunities through local, state, or federal governments. If the department decides to pursue a grant to fund the projects, the department will likely have to make a grant request in writing. The request may be very detailed, almost mirroring the methods section in a research paper.

Exercise 5.1

Identify a topic you would like to see funded through a grant. Then, research potential funding sources. You can use Grants.gov or Google foundations, state governments, and other organizations that may provide funding.

The Application Process

Since the U.S. federal government is the largest grant funding source for criminal justice, this section will focus on the common components required in requests for proposals from the federal government. Specifically, this section will focus on the application process and the writing required in the grant application.

Grants.gov is the clearinghouse website for all federal government agency grants. At Grants.gov, grant writers can find funding opportunity announcements (FOAs), search for grant opportunities, find the required application forms, and get help with grant projects. Grants.gov allows applications to be completed online and provides technical assistance to grant applicants.

Funding agencies issue an FOA once they have identified their funding priorities based on legislation and budgets. The FOA includes all information and requirements for applicants to determine their eligibility, competency, and interest in the funding opportunity (Grants.gov, n.d.-a). If an applicant decides that the FOA is suited to his or her project or study, the applicant will complete the grant application.

The grant application is submitted during the pre-award phase of the grant life cycle. According to Grants.gov (n.d.-a), the grant life cycle consists of a pre-award phase, when the agency determines the funding opportunity from its mission and objectives and announces the application process; the award phase, when reviewers evaluate the grant applications and suggest which agencies should be funded, and the agency makes the award and provides notifications to the applicants; and the postaward phase, when the federal funding office oversees the implementation, reporting, and close-out of the grant funding.

The application process requires applicants to register through Grants .gov prior to applying to an FOA. The registrations can take several weeks to process and are used to make sure the applicant and his or her agency meet at least the minimum requirements to apply for public tax dollars. Grants .gov (n.d.-a), also suggests that applicants review the websites of the primary funding agency and their community blog for additional assistance in completing the application process.

Once an application is submitted, it proceeds through several stages. The first stage is the initial screening to ensure that the application is complete. This stage is completed by the funding agency, which does not review the application for quality, only for the required material. The second stage is the programmatic review and assessment of the application for substance (Grants.gov, n.d.-a). The second stage is typically completed by outside peer reviewers with expertise in the topic area and the methodology. The reviewers are provided a numerical scoring system or uniform rating scale, and they provide comments regarding the quality of the application and the ability of the applicant to carry out the proposed idea. The third stage is the financial review of the proposed budgets. Although outside reviewers will evaluate the budget, the primary funding agency determines if the budget meets the expenses allowable for the grant. The final stage is the award decision and announcement (Grants.gov, n.d.-a).

Although this discussion only focuses on federal grants, it should be noted that grants awarded by corporations, foundations, and private individuals may not face as rigorous a review as federal grants or those coming from other government entities. However, all grant applications proceed through several steps of review prior to being awarded. The primary funding agency is most interested in funding applications that best meet the needs of the agency and have thorough and complete budgets that are mindful of costs.

Components of a Grant Application

A grant application to the federal government can be quite lengthy and relies on research, support from the literature and local statistics, and research methods and data collection. The applicant will need to be familiar with research methods in order to write a thorough and proper grant application. Since each funding agency will specify the components required for the grant application, the applicant will also want to be familiar with the format required. All guidelines provided by the funding agency must be followed, or the grant application can be disqualified (University of Southern Indiana, 2019).

Even though there may be differences in the required information from funding agency to funding agency, there are some common components required in most grant applications. These are discussed here.

Cover Page

Funding agencies usually provide the format for the cover page. They will also provide special forms for the administrative and fiscal information required in the application (University of Southern Indiana, 2019), so the applicant only needs to follow the defined format and complete the required forms. As noted in Figure 5.1, common information required on a

Figure 5.1 Sample Grant Application Cover Page

ANY GRANT SAMPLE

COVER PAGE

Name of PI: Institutional Affiliation:	Mailing Address: Phone: Email: Fax:
Name of Additional Investigator: Institutional Affiliation:	Mailing Address: Phone: Email: Fax:
Name of Administrative Official/Additional Investigator: Institutional Affiliation:	Mailing Address: Phone: Email: Fax:
Name of Grant/Project Title:	
Total Amount Requested: ($25,000–$150,000 awards available)	

*If more than 3 investigators or more than 2 administrative officials, please attach a separate sheet with each investigator's name, institutional affiliation, and contact information.

PLEASE SUBMIT THE FOLLOWING INFORMATION FOR THE GRANT APPLICATION TO BE COMPLETE:

- Cover Page
- Abstract
- Table of Contents
- Introduction
- Project Goals and Objectives
- Literature Review
- Description of Program/Project, Personnel, Methodology, Budget Narrative, etc.
- Budget
- Supplementary Materials, including curriculum vitas, letters of support, etc.

Signatures of PI, Additional Investigators, Administrative Officials and Date cover page includes the project title and summary, the total requested budget amount, the name and contact information of the primary investigator (the person planning to oversee the application process and project), the signature of the primary investigator, and the names, signatures, and contact information of any administrative officials overseeing the primary investigator (University of Southern Indiana, 2019). If additional information is requested by the funding agency, it should also be included in the cover page. If there is no defined format, it is safe to include the information provided here. As suggested by its name, the cover page should be the first page in a grant application.

Exercise 5.2

Write a cover page including the information identified here, naming yourself as the primary investigator and your professor as the administrative official. Consider what type of information you would include as contact information for both of you, what you will name your project, and how much money you may request in funding to implement the project.

Abstract or Project Summary

The abstract is written as a summary of the proposal and is included at the beginning of a grant application. Typically, the abstract or project summary immediately follows the cover page. The abstract is often publicized by the funding agency to announce successfully funded projects (University of Southern Indiana, 2019). It may also be used by outside reviewers to quickly identify what the applicant is proposing. A funding agency may provide a format for the abstract. However, if one is not provided, like the abstract for a research paper, the grant application abstract should be concise, discussing only how the application meets the grant requirements. The abstract should not be more than one or two paragraphs in length. An example of a formatted abstract is provided in Figure 5.2.

Table of Contents

Since grant applications are reviewed by representatives of the funding agency and by outside peer reviewers, they should include a table of contents. The table of contents should provide a detailed list of all topics, subtopics, illustrations, appendices, and tables (University of Southern Indiana, 2019). Like the abstract or project summary, the table of contents is provided at the beginning of the grant application.

Introduction

Most funding agencies require an introduction that states the goals of the proposed project and the timeline, and provides a background or context for the intended project (University of Southern Indiana, 2019). Figure 5.3 provides a sample introduction for a grant application. In an introduction, for

Figure 5.2 Sample Grant Abstract

ANY GRANT
SAMPLE ABSTRACT

Statement of the problem: Juvenile gangs continue to be an issue in inner-city areas. Their existence affects communities, and they are of critical concern in school safety. Stop Gangs is a threat response program in a midwestern school district that addresses the critical need for deterrence in gang recruitment and for developing school–community partnerships that discourage the range of violent gang behaviors that threaten the safety of schools.

Subjects: Nineteen schools serving K–6 graders in the Midwest will participate in a randomized, cluster sample study to examine the impact of Stop Gangs on student and community perceptions of school safety. Schools in the treatment group will participate in the Stop Gangs curriculum over a 1-year period, involving community leadership and groups, while schools in the control group will continue to use their current school safety protocol.

Partnerships: The project is being led by Any University, which will implement the project. The curriculum has been created by faculty in the School of Criminal Justice and Department of Secondary Education. Faculty will support the implementation of the Stop Gangs curriculum, manage the research portion of the project, present the findings at academic and professional conferences, and develop professional development products and tools.

Research design and methods: This project will use a randomized cluster sample to examine the Stop Gangs curriculum and its relationship to perceptions of school safety among students and community members. The study will describe current and revised school safety protocols and track juvenile arrest records and gang affiliations. Finally, the study will report the findings to stakeholders in the community and at academic and professional conferences.

Analysis: Any University will analyze all data using statistics appropriate for randomized cluster sampling and using tests of significance for the treatment effect.

Products: Any University will provide midterm and final reports to stakeholders and academic and professional community members. Any University will present a minimum of two research reports for publication and provide research briefs to share the findings. The investigators will also arrange at least one school-based informational meeting to present findings to all school personnel in the participating 19 schools. Data sets will be shared with others who are interested in the project.

example, the applicant may discuss the theory supporting the idea or success rates of similar projects in other geographical areas. The introduction sets the tone for the project (University of Southern Indiana, 2019).

Program Goals and Objectives

The goals and objectives of a grant project should be clearly identified, related to the FOA, and associated with the legislative, political, and fiscal mission of the funding agency. The goal of the program should explain what the applicant hopes to accomplish during the project. The program objectives refer to the precise outcomes of the project (University of Southern Indiana, 2019; see, e.g., Figure 5.4). For example, a grant project hoping to reduce the number of positive drug tests of probationers might state that positive drug tests while on probation will be reduced by 15% over the course of 1 year. The program objectives should also be measurable

Figure 5.3 Sample Introduction for a Grant Proposal

ANY GRANT
SAMPLE GRANT INTRODUCTION

The overall goal of Stop Gangs is to develop knowledge about how to make schools safer and to reduce gang recruitment and the violence associated with gang behaviors in schools. Juvenile gang affiliation is a continuing concern for schools nationwide. Juveniles involved in gangs are disproportionally affected by school suspensions and disciplinary referrals, have numerous negative peer relationships, and suffer long-term negative outcomes, like potential youth or adult incarceration. Compared with other schools, students in inner-city schools feel less safe at school (Allen, 2009).

Any University proposes to evaluate perceptions of school safety among inner-city youth in 19 midwestern K–6 schools. Randomized cluster samples will be used to implement curriculum designed to decrease gang involvement and recruitment, strengthen perceptions of safety in school, and promote stronger antigang relationships between schools and communities. The intent is to identify school safety protocol that reduces gang involvement and recruitment and decreases violent behaviors in schools prompted by gang members.

In order to be successful in reducing gang involvement and school violence related to gang membership, schools must be committed to providing safe and nurturing environments. To reduce gang membership and involvement, teachers should be provided training on managing disruptive students, and schools should soften or eliminate zero-tolerance policies to reduce suspensions and expulsions, provide tutoring for poorly performing students, provide training in interpersonal skills in conflict resolution, provide training for school resource officers in mediating conflicts, and provide gang awareness training for school personnel, parents, and students (Youth.gov, n.d.).

Figure 5.4 Sample Program Objectives

ANY GRANT SAMPLE
PROGRAM OBJECTIVES

The proposed program has the following three objectives:

1. To implement the Stop Gangs curriculum in a randomized, cluster sample of schools in the Midwest over a 1-year period.

2. To explore the impact and outcome of the Stop Gangs curriculum on reducing gang involvement among youth in midwestern schools over a 1-year period.

3. To explore the impact and outcome of the Stop Gangs curriculum on violent behaviors of youth in midwestern schools over a 1-year period.

and supportive of the program goals. When writing the program goals and objectives, it is recommended that applicants use the SMART approach (specific, measurable, allocable, reasonable, and timely) (University of Southern Indiana, 2019).

Identify one program goal and one related program objective for a grant application proposing a cyber bullying prevention program in elementary schools.

Review of the Literature

Federal government grants and many other types of grants require the applicant to provide a literature review. In this review, the applicant should discuss the work done by others with similar programs, theories supporting the project idea and implementation, and findings from studies related to the proposed idea. In the literature review, the applicant can identify how his or her project is similar to as well as different from other related projects and studies (University of Southern Indiana, 2019).

Description of the Proposed Project

The project description is the foundation of the entire grant application. This is where the applicant provides the needs statement and the road map for how the project will commence, progress, and conclude. Typically, the FOA will provide general instructions for the types of topics to discuss in the description of the proposed project, but it is up to the applicant to provide the detailed information. According to the University of Southern Indiana (2019, n.p.), the description of the proposed project should focus, at a minimum, on the following:

- Establish the need for the project and the benefits derived.

- Be realistic. Distinguish between long-range goals and the short-range objectives for which funding is being sought.

- Develop a clear timeline for your objectives.

- Clearly define the focus of the project, including its limits.

- Clearly identify the means of evaluating the data or the conclusions.

- Clearly describe the connection between the objectives and the methods to show that the approach is carefully developed and thought out.

Plan of Action, Methodology, and Design

This section of a grant proposal provides very specific details on the steps and procedures that will be used to measure success in the project (evaluation) and how long the project will take to complete (University of Southern Indiana, 2019). In this section, there is often a required visual illustration of the timeline, a logic model showing progression and measurements, as well as clear descriptions of how personnel will accomplish the goals and objectives. Funding agencies may also expect that the project will continue after the funding period has ended. In this case, it is appropriate for an applicant to provide information on how the project will be supported at the conclusion of the funding period or if the study or project will end then.

Personnel

Grant funders always require a detailed description of the personnel working with a grant. This includes, many times, job descriptions, hire dates, whether a person is full-time or part-time, the education and background of the person, the person's specific expertise in the project, and his or her resume. Since a grant is an investment by the funding agency, the agency will want to ensure that the research team is capable and willing to contribute to the study (University of Southern Indiana, 2019). An example explanation of capabilities and job duties is given in Figure 5.5. Often, specific individuals are already identified as personnel when the proposal is submitted, but they do not have to be. In some grant applications, the applicant can propose a position without identifying a specific person to fill that position. It is also possible for applicants to use consultants who only contribute to limited portions of the project and will not be employed for the duration of the funded period.

Budget

When writing the budget for a grant application, the applicant must not only provide a written narrative that explains the various expenses and why

Figure 5.5 Sample Explanation of Capabilities and Job Duties

ANY GRANT SAMPLE
EXPLANATION OF CAPABILITIES AND JOB DUTIES

A qualified professor, (insert name, if known), PhD, will be the project director for the Stop Gangs grant. Dr. (insert name) has over 20 years of experience in teaching and research on U.S. and foreign-based gangs. He has worked with multiple police departments to successfully implement gang programming and gang units. Under his direction, gang rates in several urban areas have decreased by 3%, and he has written multiple best-practice articles for government agencies and academic journals.

Dr. (insert name) has received training from the FBI on gang suppression and removal. He currently serves on a Threat Assessment Regional Team on gang suppression. Dr. (insert name) oversees all gang curriculum within the School of Justice at Any University. Dr. (insert name) was instrumental in the development of the Stop Gangs curriculum with the faculty in the Department of Secondary Education.

He will oversee all programmatic and operational activities of the grant. He will oversee the faculty, staff, and teachers involved in the implementation and teaching of the Stop Gangs curriculum. He will also oversee the grant's financial integrity and approve all contracts and research studies.

Dr. (insert name) will handle all marketing and community outreach as well as spearhead the reports and presentations to stakeholders.

Dr. (insert name) has been the primary investigator on two other gang-based grants at the federal and state levels. He has also served as an additional investigator on a curriculum development and training grant in gang suppression.

they are necessary but also complete the required formatted budget sheet or provide a spreadsheet or table with the budget expenses listed (University of Southern Indiana, 2019). An example budget can be found in Figure 5.6. Although the narrative can be brief (one or two pages), the applicant should be sure to explain all the budgeted items. If more space is needed, it is better to extend the narrative than not discuss why the applicant is requesting a trip, tangible item, or person. If the grant applicant has additional support from another grant or a corporation, an individual, or the applicant's own agency (as in-kind revenue), the applicant should identify these sources and

Figure 5.6 Sample Numerical and Narrative Budget for a Grant

ANY GRANT SAMPLE
NUMERICAL BUDGET AND BUDGET NARRATIVE

A budget will be presented in both numerical and narrative form.

Budget Category	Budget Amount Requested
Personnel	$61,792.00
Fringe benefits	$38,693.00
Travel	$3,687.00
Equipment	$2,974.00
Supplies	$497.00
Construction	$0
Consultants and contracts	$78,945.00
Other	$28,567.00
Total requested amount	$215,155.00

Once the numerical budget is presented, the narrative will be used to describe each item listed on the numerical budget. Although not all listed items are described, some of the narrative items are exampled here.

Personnel
Personnel costs reflect the current salary for each position based on the time each person will spend on the Stop Gangs curriculum implementation and teaching. Personnel include a project director (0.75 FTE), a project coordinator (0.50 FTE), teacher supervisors (2 × 0.025 FTE), and school police officers (1 × 0.50 FTE).

Fringe benefits
Fringe benefit costs reflect the rates for each classification of employee. Benefits include Medicare, Social Security, Unemployment Tax, Workers Compensation, and Health and Welfare.

Supplies
Supply costs include general office supplies at $150.00 and marketing supplies for outreach, education, and awareness at $347.00. Marketing supplies include brochures, posters, banners, T-shirts, and mailings to community members.

the potential resources being provided. In some cases, a funding agency may expect matching funds from the applicant agency or in-kind donations of some type to assist with the project. This type of support is viewed as a commitment by the agency to the proposed project. The budget narrative is often provided within the body of the grant application, while the budget sheet is included as an appendix.

Dissemination of Findings

Findings from federally funded grants are often summarized and disseminated to agencies or organizations in criminal justice, the health services, and other disciplines. Thus, it is important for applicants to develop a dissemination plan describing how they will let "the wider community know about the final outcomes" of the project (University of Southern Indiana, 2019, n.p.). As mentioned, funded projects are an investment, and funding agencies want to see a return on their investment. Publicity for the funding agency, changed policies, statutory changes, and so on can result from disseminated information and are viewed as significant to funding agencies.

Supplementary Materials

At the end of the grant application are included appendices, proposed personnel resumes, job descriptions, letters of support from stakeholders, and information on resources and facilities, where appropriate (University of Southern Indiana, 2019).

Additional Grant-Writing Suggestions

Of note here is that the grant applicant should be as thorough as possible in each section. Even if the funding agency limits the number of pages to be submitted—as often occurs with federal grants—the applicant must write with brevity while being comprehensive and covering all the required topics. The applicant should also write in a way that makes sense and allows for the application to flow from one topic to another. Keeping the topic order provided in this chapter may not be necessary or appropriate, so the grant applicant should consider the best order for the proposed project.

The grant application must represent the applicant's best writing. If the application is full of grammar errors, methodology errors, or budget errors, the reviewers and the funding agency may disregard it. Consider the application from the reader's perspective. Writing errors in the application are indicative of writing errors in future grant reports and in the publication materials that emerge from the dissemination plan. As with all writing, a grant application should follow standard writing rules, using the first-person point of view, the active voice, double-spacing, and flawless spelling, punctuation, and grammar. The application should be written for both an expert and an inexperienced audience, clearly explaining the intended project. Finally, grant applicants should use style rules common to their discipline (e.g., American Psychological Association [APA] formatting in criminal justice writing) when structuring the grant application. When in doubt, the applicant should always reach out to the funding agency to answer questions regarding the FOA and/or the format of the grant application.

Grant Template

The following grant template includes the major sections of a grant proposal. Please note that this sample is meant to be informative and has been edited to save space. It is not meant to represent a complete proposal that a student or criminal justice professional might submit for review.

Example 5.3   Sample Grant Template

This section provides a general template for a federal law enforcement grant proposal. Additional information on federal grant applications can be found in the *2019 OJP Grant Application Resource Guide* (Office of Justice Programs, 2018) and at https://www.grants.gov/web/grants/applicants/apply-for-grants.html (Grants.gov, n.d.-b).

1. *Application for Federal Assistance form:* Federal grant applications require using a standard government form as a cover sheet for grant applications.

2. *Executive summary:* An executive summary is written as an abstract, discussed earlier in this chapter. The executive summary summarizes the proposed project in about 400 words or less. It is written for a general public audience and is single-spaced, using standard 12-point font with a 1-inch margin (Office of Justice Programs, 2019).

3. *Problem statement/need description:* This section very concisely identifies the problem or need the funding will address. It identifies the precise purpose of the particular project and the crimes that it will address. The problem statement includes a review of specific data on the current needs of the applying law enforcement and criminal justice agencies and demonstrates how these needs can be met through the project (Office of Justice Programs, 2019).

4. *Work schedule:* The work schedule is a detailed calendar that identifies the timeline of the project. The work schedule should include milestones, deliverables, and the details of the person who is responsible for each activity (Office of Justice Programs, 2019).

5. *Budget:* The budget identifies the financials of the project, including equipment, supplies, workspace, and salaries/benefits. "Budget narratives should demonstrate generally how applicants will maximize cost effectiveness of grant expenditures" (Office of Justice Programs, 2019, n.p.).

6. *Qualifications:* This section fully describes the applicant's qualifications to carry out the grant project. If applicable, it may also include the skills of grant staff and others assigned to the project. This section will identify those who are critical to the successful completion of the project, and discuss their roles, responsibilities, and qualifications (Office of Justice Programs, 2019).

7. *Appendices/supporting materials:* Documents required by the grant solicitation are included in this section. These documents may include memoranda of understanding or interagency agreements, letters of support or collaboration, or applicable state or local laws (Office of Justice Programs, 2019).

CHAPTER SUMMARY

Criminal justice students and researchers will often find it necessary to write abstracts and proposals. An abstract is a brief summary of a report, article, speech, or book. A proposal is used to detail a research or writing project before the project begins. Writers should follow standard style rules, unless, for example, a grant solicitation specifies formatting and writing rules. Individuals writing grant applications should always consider the funding agency's mission, politics, and fiscal priorities. Grant applications should focus on the FOA and include all the requirements identified by the funding agency. Keeping grant applications thorough but concise is important, as is ensuring that the application is well written and error free, and meets the guidelines of the grant announcement and the agency's requirements. When questions arise about the process, the FOA, or the format of the grant application, the applicant should always contact the funding agency for additional information.

As with any writing project, abstracts and proposals should always represent the writer's best writing skills. An abstract may be the only part of a report that is read if it does not contain sufficient details and information to persuade the reader to read the full report. Similarly, a poorly written proposal may cause a research project to be denied or a grant proposal to go unfunded.

QUESTIONS FOR CONSIDERATION

1. Using a paper you have written as source material, write a critical, descriptive, and informative abstract for it.

2. When writing a grant proposal, why is it important to write to a general audience?

3. Imagine that you intend to write a research proposal for a project in which you will observe human participants. How might you locate and identify the participants? How will you protect them from harm? Write a one-page paper, "Participants for the Study," to address these questions.

4. Write a literature review using one source from a previous or current research project.

5. What components are typically required in a grant application?

6. Why is it important to ensure that a grant application is error free?

6 Academic Paper Formats

What Is APA Formatting?

College students are regularly asked to complete research papers in classes. The course instructor's directives for the paper probably require that students use academic formatting, most specifically American Psychological Association (APA) format. APA format is the accepted academic format for criminal justice writing. Students who become proficient in APA formatting while in college often find that they continue to use this approach when writing grants, reports, program evaluations, and other documents in their professional careers in criminal justice.

This chapter reviews the necessity for APA formatting in academic projects and discusses the types of manuscripts one is likely to see utilizing APA format, ethics and legal issues in writing and publishing, and plagiarism. Other formats, specifically the Modern Language Association (MLA) and the *Chicago Manual of Style (CMOS)*, are briefly mentioned since students may be exposed to these styles as well.

Research, Publication, and the APA Style Rules

When someone decides to analyze data or complete a research project on a specific phenomenon, he or she becomes a researcher. That researcher's work or report may be relevant to the field of study where the phenomenon exists; thus, the researcher is expected to share the completed work with others. In doing so, the researcher expands the wealth of knowledge available to other scholars and practitioners and builds upon what is already known about a specific discipline and what may still need to be investigated. Their work provides new insight on a specific phenomenon and allows others to critically assess the research, expand it, complete future projects that do not repeat the same mistakes, and contribute something new to the field of study (APA, 2010). However, in order for the work to be completely communicated to others, there has to be a standard way of writing. This is where the APA format becomes important.

The American Psychological Association created the APA format in 1929 as a method whereby researchers could formally communicate scientific research results in publications (APA, 2010). The goal was to provide a set of procedures, or style rules, that codify the format of scientific research papers to simplify reading comprehension (VandenBos, 2010). The association has revised the APA style many times, and it often includes the input of psychologists, anthropologists, and business managers. The association also consults with other researchers in the social and behavioral sciences when determining updates to the style. The current format (7th edition) provided by the APA was developed in consultation with the Publication Manual Task Force, APA members at professional meetings, and APA boards and committees, which include students (APA, 2010). The style rules consist of instructions on formatting manuscripts, tables, figures, citations, and references, and the organization of papers as well as grammar and other basic information on the mechanics of writing. Some basic style guidelines from the APA manual are provided in Box 6.1 (APA, 2010).

Box 6.1
Basic Style Rules for APA Citations

APA requires resources to be cited both in the text of the document and at the end of a document, called a reference list. APA provides very extensive citation guidelines and rules for many types of sources in their style manual. Where they do not provide a style guideline for a source, students are encouraged to choose a sample style as similar to their source as they can. Although there are no standard citation rules for all sources, some basic guidelines are provided below:

In-Text Citations

- Writers should use past tense when referring to previous research completed by authors (e.g., Smith found).

- In-text citations should immediately follow the sentence where the information was paraphrased and/or quoted.

- Writers should follow the author–date style when citing sources in the text of a document (e.g., Smith, 2018).

- When directly quoting from a source, writers should provide the author's last name, date of publication, and a page number for the source where the information came from (e.g., Smith, 2017, p. 135).

- Writers should place the punctuation mark after the in-text citation.

- Writers should capitalize proper nouns, titles, and the first word after a colon or dash in an in-text citation.

- Writers should italicize the names of longer works if the work is used in the in-text citation instead of an author's name.

- Writers should put quotation marks around titles of journal articles, television shows, song titles, and articles from edited collections.

- Writers should use special style rules for quotations that are 40 or more words that include indenting the quotation by 5 spaces, omitting the quotation marks, starting the quotation on a new line, and placing the page number at the end of the quotation and after the punctuation mark.

The Reference List

- The reference list should appear at the end of the document and begin on a new page labeled "References" in the center of the page.

- Each resource cited in the document and in in-text citations should appear in the reference list.

- Writers should double-space references.

- If a reference is longer than one line, the second line should be indented five spaces as a hanging indentation.

- Writers should provide an author's last name first followed by the author's first and middle initials.

- All authors up to and including seven authors should be provided in the reference.

(Continued)

(Continued)

Any authors after six should be indicated with an ellipsis except for the final author name, which should be included.

- Writers should alphabetize the references and use chronological order for multiple articles by the same author.

- Writers should italicize book titles, but not italicize, underline, or put quotation marks around titles of journal articles.

- Writers should provide the title in full.

- Writers should keep the punctuation and capitalization provided in a journal's name.

- Writers should capitalize the first letter in the first word of a title and subtitle, the first letter in the first word after a colon or dash, and proper nouns.

Source: Adapted from Purdue University (2018). The Purdue online writing lab. Retrieved from https://owl.purdue.edu/.

Why Use a Style Guide?

Often, students ask why there is an emphasis on writing style versus a simple focus on grammar and proper English. VandenBos (2010, p. xiv), stated,

> Uniform style helps us to cull articles quickly for key points and findings. Rules of style in scientific writing encourage full disclosure of essential information and allow us to dispense with minor distractions. Style helps us express the key elements of quantitative results, choose the graphic form that will best suit our analyses, report critical details of our research protocol, and describe individuals with accuracy and respect.

All of this clears the way for researchers to focus on the substance of their research, rather than the writing style (VandenBos, 2010).

Having a set of style rules also provides a formal system for journals, books, and other media to follow when publishing the work of researchers. Print media and digital media may require a researcher to format their work according to the APA style rules. In doing so, the work can be more easily read and reviewed by other scholars and those interested in the study. Box 6.2 provides general guidelines for information included in APA-formatted references.

Box 6.2
General Information Included in APA-Formatted References

1. Author's name(s) written with last name first, followed by first initial and middle initial

2. Year of publication in parentheses

3. Title of book, article, paper, etc.

4. Journal name italicized (omitted if not a journal)

5. Volume number of the journal or edition of the book

6. Issue number of the journal in parentheses (omitted if not a journal)

7. Page numbers where article is printed within the journal (omitted if not a journal)

Additionally, legitimizing the research is a requirement of the scientific research community. This usually involves a review of the manuscript by other experts familiar with the discipline who peer-review (or referee) the paper for theory, methods, data, and analysis. The reviewers assess the strength of the project in following the scientific protocol of research. They determine the strengths and weaknesses of the manuscript, which should also be provided by the researcher in the paper, and consider the rigor of the design, methodology, analysis, interpretation of the data, and reporting. Reviewers also verify the transparency of the study's details so that others may reproduce or extend the findings (National Institutes of Health, 2017). Reviews that end in positive appraisals are published, while those manuscripts that are reviewed negatively may need to be rewritten or revised to meet the standards of the scientific community. If reviewers conclude the manuscript has serious scientific, ethical, or legal flaws, the study may never be published.

Types of Publications

Journals

If a study is published, it may appear in a journal. Students are often familiar with journals because they do online and in-person library searches for articles on various topics when writing research papers. Journals come in a variety of formats (print and digital), as well as refereed and non-refereed. A refereed journal will use the peer-reviewed practice described above, while a nonrefereed journal may publish articles that have only been reviewed by an editor or an editorial board who may or may not have knowledge and experience related to the reviewed article's topic. In this case, the article may be reviewed more for style and formatting than for scientific and academic validity.

Scholarly or refereed journals publish articles that are considered primary or original works and may consist of "empirical studies, literature reviews, theoretical articles, methodological articles, or case studies" (APA, 2010, p. 9). Empirical studies are original research projects that include secondary data analysis, testing hypotheses, and presentations of new data that may not have been presented in previous research studies. Literature reviews, which are most familiar to students, include synthesizing and critically evaluating previously published studies on a specific phenomenon (APA, 2010). Theoretical articles use existing publications to advance theory by reviewing the theory from development through time pointing out flaws and/or adding to or modifying the theory. Methodological articles present new methods of analysis, modify existing methods, and/or discuss quantitative and analytical approaches to data. They may rely on "highly technical materials" (APA, 2010, p. 11) and appeal to more experienced researchers. Finally, case studies are reports that illustrate a problem, provide solutions to the problem, and highlight the need for additional research on the problem, clinical applications, or theory related to the problem (APA, 2010). Other types of articles published in scholarly journals may include book reviews, letters to the editor, brief reports, program analyses, and monographs. These types of articles are usually refereed, or reviewed, by experts in the discipline of study. There is a plethora of these journals in criminal justice, but a few examples include *Youth and Society*, *Deviant Behavior*, *Criminal Justice and Behavior*, and *Criminology, Criminal Justice, Law & Society*.

It should also be noted that the term *journal* in the title of a publication does not necessarily indicate it is refereed (University of Washington–Tacoma, 2018). Nonrefereed or edited articles may appear in journals in print and online. Trade journals are usually considered nonrefereed or edited and are written by and for professionals in a particular field or industry. These types of journals are useful for content on current practices and programs in criminal justice and other professions (University of Washington–Tacoma, 2018). As stated previously, nonrefereed or edited journals use editors or editorial boards to review article submissions from authors. The editor or editorial board may or may not be familiar with the article's topic and typically review articles for grammar, relevance, timeliness, and style. If the article is seen as meeting the criteria, an editor can choose to publish the article in a nonrefereed journal. Although not the gold standard of publications, some articles found in edited journals are well written and contribute to the field or discipline in some meaningful way, such as those found in trade journals. However, students should not rely on these types of journals for solid, scientific content. A couple examples of edited journals include *Corrections Today* and the *FBI Law Enforcement Bulletin*.

Magazines

Magazines fall into the nonrefereed or edited category. Magazines are written for a general audience and do not necessarily follow academic style rules, such as APA formatting. Magazines may publish articles on many topics in one edition and may have paid advertising space for various products and services. Magazines are abridged, and the determination of what to publish is decided by an editor. Articles found in magazines are assumed to be factually correct but may contain errors and be written for universal appeal rather than truth. Examples of magazines include *Police Chief*, *US News and World Report*, and *Newsweek*, among others.

Government Publications

Government publications tend to follow the style rules of the APA. Government publications typically are produced by the U.S. federal government or a foreign government. The Department of Justice publishes the majority of articles in the United States related to criminal justice, although some other departments within the federal government write articles or do studies in criminal justice too. Government publications are considered legitimate, academic (or scholarly) sources. They are reviewed by scholars in the field and undergo a rigorous editing process. Students can find government articles by searching federal government websites or using Google to search a broad topic. Google can limit the topic search to only governmental websites if *.gov* is added to the search bar. The Department of Homeland Security, Office of Juvenile Justice and Delinquency Prevention, Uniform Crime Reports, and National Institute of Justice Publications are a few federal departments that students can use to find articles related to criminal justice topics. Of course, there are many other federal departments and websites as well.

Books

Finally, books are often used as references in student research projects. Books are not refereed by experts in the field, though they may be reviewed by individuals with knowledge in the subject area. Typically, publishers, like Sage or McGraw-Hill, commission authors to write books and guarantee the authors lump sum payments or royalties from the sale of the book. The authors may write the entire book, portions of a book, or only single chapters. Books can be used as legitimate references for research projects, but they are considered secondary sources, not primary. In most cases, students should seek primary or refereed journal articles to supplement their work and not rely solely on books.

In summary, APA formatting will likely be used in almost all publications discussed in this section. APA formatting can help students decide how much authority to afford to a particular publication. If the publication follows rigid APA style and the articles in the publication are found to be

"WHAT I CALLED CREATIVE RECYCLING
THE SCHOOL CALLED PLAGIARISM."

Source: Used with permission from T- (Theresa) McCracken.

refereed, the student can rest assured that the information is well founded in scientific protocol. However, if the publication provides a mix of styles or little APA formatting, the student should likely question the contents of the work. Comprehending that APA formatting provides a way for authors to communicate ideas and research clearly to one another is significant in understanding a student's need to learn and use APA style rules. In addition to the communication goal, APA formatting plays a part in ethical and legal standards in publishing. In the next section of this chapter, ethical and legal standards are discussed in relation to APA formatting and publications.

APA Formatting and Ethical and Legal Standards

Following legal and ethical standards in writing is a requirement of scientific researchers. If a researcher fails to follow ethical guidelines set forth by the discipline, he or she may face scrutiny, the research may be disregarded, and the researcher's reputation may not recover, which would dampen future projects. Legally, a researcher is required to follow statutes governing research and, in the case of using human subjects, may have to get permission for the research from the federal office of Human Subjects Protections, the researcher's agency, or an educational institution's Institutional Review Board (IRB), which governs the legitimacy of research. Knowing and understanding these expectations is extremely important for the scholarly researcher and will be discussed in the following paragraphs.

Ethics

Merriam-Webster's Dictionary (2018) defines *ethics* as a set of moral principles. It is assumed that these moral principles guide an individual's behavior by helping them to determine right from wrong. Ethics are usually learned from the family, in school, in church, or in other social settings (Resnick, 2015). Groups can also have ethics or principles that guide their approach to moral issues or situations and provide a philosophy specifying how they will behave. This group philosophy is known as professional ethics when it governs behavior in a particular profession. Psychologists, doctors, police officers, and many other professions practice professional ethics. Scholarly researchers also use professional ethics founded in scientific protocol and recognized by the APA.

Just as ethics govern the behavior of professions and "establish the public's trust in the discipline" (Resnick, 2015, Para. 6), ethics in research accomplish five main goals: (1) Ethics promote knowledge, truth, and the avoidance of error; (2) ethics promote collaboration in research; (3) ethics hold researchers accountable for their work and to the public; (4) ethics build public support for the importance of research; and (5) ethics promote other social and moral causes such as human rights, legal compliance, and animal safety, to name a few (Resnick, 2015, Paras. 7–11). Thus, given the importance of ethics in research, it is expected that all researchers will be familiar with and adhere to the ethical standards identified within their discipline or profession and within the scientific protocol when conducting research. Typically, the researcher can find these ethical expectations in their professional code of ethics and/or on government websites that provide research ethics. Box 6.3 shows the professional code of ethics for probation and pre-trial services officers stated on Federal Probation and Pre-Trial Officers Association website. The professional code of ethics for research is provided in Table 6.1 from the National Institute of Health.

Box 6.3
Federal Probation and Pre-Trial Officers Association Code of Ethics

AS A FEDERAL PROBATION/PRETRIAL SERVICES OFFICER,

I AM DEDICATED TO RENDERING PROFESSIONAL SERVICE to the Courts, the parole authorities and the community at large in effecting the social adjustment of the offender and assuring the compliance of defendants with their legal responsibilities.

I WILL CONDUCT MY PERSONAL LIFE WITH DECORUM, will neither accept nor grant favors in connection with my office, and will put loyalty to moral principles above personal consideration.

I WILL UPHOLD THE LAW WITH DIGNITY and with complete awareness of the prestige and stature of the judicial system of which I am a part. I will be ever cognizant of my responsibility to the community which I serve.

I WILL STRIVE TO BE OBJECTIVE IN THE PERFORMANCE OF MY DUTIES, respect the inalienable rights of all persons, appreciate the inherent worth of the individual, and inviolate those confidences which can be reposed in me.

I WILL COOPERATE WITH MY FELLOW WORKERS AND RELATED AGENCIES and will continually attempt to improve my professional standards through the seeking of knowledge and understanding.

I RECOGNIZE MY OFFICE AS A SYMBOL OF PUBLIC FAITH and I accept it as a public trust to be held as long as I am true to the ethics of the Federal Probation and Pre-trial Services System. I will constantly strive to achieve these objectives and ideals, dedicating myself to my chosen profession.
Revised March 11, 1993

Source: Federal Probation and Pre-Trial Officers Association. (2018). Code of Ethics. Retrieved from www .fppoa.org/page/code-ethics. Reprinted with permission from the FPPOA.

Table 6.1   Shared Values in Scientific Research

Honesty	convey information truthfully and honoring commitments
Accuracy	report findings precisely and take care to avoid errors
Efficiency	use resources wisely and avoid waste
Objectivity	let the facts speak for themselves and avoid improper bias

Source: Steneck, N. H. (2007). *ORI—Introduction to the Responsible Conduct of Research*, Washington DC, U.S. Government Printing Office.

Introduction to the Responsible Conduct of Research

Ethics in scientific protocol provides basic standards for all researchers to follow when conducting and presenting research. According to scientific protocol (Smith, 2003), when completing ethical research projects, researchers should do the following:

1. *Be truthful in discussing intellectual property.* Researchers should discuss who gets credit for the work, how authors' names will appear on projects, and what work will be done by each participant. Faculty, independent researchers, and students who share in the responsibility of contributing to the conceptualization of the project, development and completion of the project, and distribution of the research deserve authorship and acknowledgment. Researchers also need to fulfill the ethical obligation of correcting research errors and/or allowing others to duplicate the research using the same data.

2. *Understand roles.* It is important for researchers to realize they play multiple roles in relationships. For example, a teacher who uses students in experiments may unintentionally violate the student's right to say no to the project because the student may feel pressured: If they don't participate, their grade may be affected. Research participation should be voluntary for subjects. So, researchers should not take advantage of their professional role in pursuing research or research participants, and should realize that the multiple roles they play in relationships with others could create a harmful or unethical environment for research.

3. *Show respect for persons.* As mentioned above, participants in research projects should participate voluntarily and without fear of harm. Research participants should know and understand the risks and benefits of the research, the purpose of the research, the expectations on their time and involvement, their ability to withdraw or refuse to participate, how their information and contributions will be identified, analyzed, and dispersed, if incentives are available for their participation, and who to contact if they experience discomfort or have questions. Researchers should get consent to participate in research in writing from subjects and should continually assess the research to ensure it is not harming participants beyond what was identified at the beginning of the project.

4. *Protect confidentiality and privacy.* Like doctors are required to secure medical records, researchers have an ethical responsibility to protect the responses and identity of those who participate in research projects. Researchers should discuss with participants how their identity will be protected and when or if their information will be shared in publications or presentations.

Researchers should talk to subjects about the harms they may experience as a result of their participation and should strive to eliminate as many of those harms as possible by securing the identity of research subjects. If a subject's name or other identifying information cannot be anonymous, the researcher should design a system to secure their data in locked cabinets or behind security passwords on electronic devices. These procedures should be shared with the subjects, and their consent to participate once knowing the risk should be secured prior to involvement in the research project.

5. *Use other ethical resources.* A researcher should know and understand state and federal laws with regard to research and using human subjects in research. Additionally, a researcher should get permission for the research from their IRB if one is available or through the federal Office of Human Subjects Protections.

In addition to the ethical guidelines above, the APA requires the open sharing of data among researchers. They suggest that researchers maintain their secured data for a minimum of 5 years. This allows other researchers to request permission to view or verify the data. It also allows for questions to be answered with respect to the accuracy of the data, analysis, and publication (APA, 2010). The APA provides further guidelines on publishing data, duplicating work in multiple journals or articles (this should be avoided), and publishing data piecemeal or parsing out data in various publications. Accordingly, the APA prohibits researchers from misrepresenting data from its original format and publishing the same data or idea in two separate sources. The association believes this gives "the erroneous impression that findings are more replicable than is the case or that particular conclusions are more strongly supported than is warranted by cumulative evidence" (APA, 2010, p. 13). Piecemeal publications, or unnecessarily splitting the findings across multiple articles, is also discouraged by APA because it can "be misleading if multiple reports appear to represent independent instances of data collection or analyses" (p. 14) and the scientific literature, as a whole, could be distorted. Of course, there may be times that an author must limit the amount of findings presented in a single article because of journal constraints or because the research project is ongoing. In these instances, the researchers should acknowledge any previous work using the data or idea both in the article as well as in discussions with the journal or book editor. Not doing so could result in legal as well as ethical challenges for the authors. Both copyright laws and plagiarism, which will be discussed, apply in these cases.

Discussing ethical responsibilities and understanding the potential ethical violations that may occur in a project beforehand is good practice for researchers. Being familiar with federal mandates on research ethics, like those from the National Institutes of Health, manuals, like the APA Manual (2010), and documents like *The Belmont Report*, a 1979 report from the

National Commission for the Protection of Human Subjects of Biomedical and Behavioral Research, which discussed ethical practices in using human subjects and is still the basis for ethical practices in research involving human subjects, are key in avoiding ethical violations and determining how best to handle those that may occur.

Notice that being truthful is an essential element of research. For those researchers that choose not to follow ethical guidelines, legal issues may arise.

Legal Aspects

Writers must also be aware of legal issues that govern publications. Copyright and fair use laws, plagiarism, and protecting the health and welfare of research subjects are some of the legal concerns that researchers must consider when completing papers, presentations, research projects, and other works. As discussed in Chapter 2, copyright and fair use laws are federal laws governed by the U.S. Copyright Office and apply to original works. You will likely recall that these statutes do not apply to ideas, facts, systems, or methods of operation. One example of a common copyright error made by students is to copy and paste charts or graphs from outside sources into their work. This is inappropriate since the chart or graph is likely copyrighted. Using the original work or paraphrasing (i.e., summarizing in their own words) the original work without giving credit to the author is a potential violation of copyright laws and could possibly result in a lawsuit by the original author. If proper credit, such as citations and references, are provided acknowledging where the information came from, the student is typically on safe ground.

Fair use laws are part of the copyright law that allows nonprofit and educational institutions to reproduce original works, develop spin-offs of original works, and distribute copies of original works through sale or lease. Fair use laws also control public domain information. Public domain information includes material with expired, forfeited, or waived property rights, and where property rights do not apply, such as in government documents. Finding oneself in violation of any of the copyright laws or clauses could result in a number of legal penalties, to include fines ranging from $200 to $150,000 for each violation, an actual dollar amount for damages, having to pay attorney fees and court fees, jail, impounding of the illegal work, and injunctions (Purdue University, n.d.). Since student writers and researchers often do not have the resources to pay fines and court costs, providing credit when credit is due is the easiest way to avoid copyright infringements. Additionally, it is an ethical requirement. Aside from civil and criminal legal ramifications, it is considered plagiarism to not provide credit to original authors.

Plagiarism

Although there are no state or federal laws against plagiarism, there can be consequences for plagiarizing and, in extreme cases, civil liability may be one result. Plagiarism is using the words or ideas of another without affording proper credit to the original author. The APA Ethics Code Standard 8.11, forbids authors from claiming the words or ideas of another as their own (APA, 2010). Using only a few words, full sentences, or entire works in a paper or presentation without affording the original author the credit makes it appear that the writer created the work. This is an example of plagiarism. Self-plagiarism is also unethical and includes using previously published or submitted work as new scholarship. For example, a student who submits a paper in one class that was already submitted and graded in another class commits self-plagiarism. In yet another example, an author who submits a previously published article to a different journal has committed self-plagiarism. To avoid self-plagiarism "the core of the new document must constitute an original contribution to the knowledge, and only the amount of previously published material necessary to understand that contribution should be included [in the new work]" (APA, 2010, p. 16). Additionally, when using previously published or submitted work, the author's own words should be cited, and references should be made to the fact that the work was used previously. The writer should say things like "as I stated previously" or "as I published previously" to inform the readers that the material has been used before. The writer should also provide in-text citations that include his or her own name and the date the previous paper or article was published or submitted.

Committing plagiarism can result in hefty consequences. In 2003, a news reporter from the *New York Times*, Jayson Blair, was accused of plagiarizing 36 of the 73 articles he wrote for the newspaper. He copied words or stories from other news outlets, faked photos, committed self-plagiarism, and made up facts and quotes in many of the stories (CNN .com, 2003). As a result of his transgressions, he was fired from the newspaper and a very public investigation and article appeared in the paper describing what he had done. Blair has never worked in journalism again (CNN.com, 2003). Other cases of plagiarism have resulted in similar fates for journalists and book authors. One book author, Kaavya Viswanathan, was accused of plagiarizing portions of her book from other authors in the same genre and had a book deal worth more than half a million dollars revoked (Bailey, 2012). Viswanathan also changed careers as a result of the accusations. Students in college who commit plagiarism may also face severe penalties that include zero grades on papers or projects, referrals to academic dishonesty investigatory boards within the university, failing a class, and/or expulsion from the university, depending on the severity of the plagiarism. Box 6.4 presents Harvard University's student code of conduct with regard to plagiarism. Notice that the university refers to plagiarism as academic dishonesty and places the responsibility for upholding academic integrity upon the student. This is common practice for all writers, regardless of status (e.g., researchers, faculty, authors, students). It is the author, not the publisher, who is responsible for avoiding plagiarism.

Box 6.4
Tips to Avoid Plagiarism

Writers are required to differentiate their own words from those of others. They are required to format papers in such a way that a reader can identify a source used by the writer and to format information according to standard style rules. These style rules include APA, MLA, or *Chicago Manual of Style* guidelines.

It is considered plagiarism if a writer fails to acknowledge the work of another, claims—intentionally or unintentionally—the words or ideas of another, incorporates facts from another's work, or uses language written by another without providing the proper credit to the original author (Harvard Extension School, 2017–2018). Plagiarism in an academic environment can result in very serious consequences.

Harvard University places responsibility for avoiding and for identifying plagiarism on both faculty and students. Students are responsible for knowing and understanding the policies on academic integrity and for using sources in responsible ways. Harvard does not provide leniency for students who claim not to understand the rules and for those that "fail to uphold academic integrity" (Harvard Extension School, 2017–2018). Faculty are also responsible for paying close attention to work submitted by students and reporting violations of academic integrity and cheating to the dean of students.

Harvard, like many other schools, provides failing course grades for students who violate cheating and plagiarism policies.

They may also suspend students for one academic year.

According to the Harvard Extension School (2017–2018), students can use the following tips to avoid plagiarism:

1. Cite all sources—this includes primary and secondary sources as well as online, open source, and instructor lectures.

2. Make sure to understand the assignment and its requirements—make sure the instructor wants outside sources to be included in the assignment and make sure to use the proper citation style.

3. Do not procrastinate—waiting to the last minute to complete the assignment may allow for citation mistakes to occur. Work ahead and take the time necessary to avoid plagiarism.

4. Make sure to include all sources and be thorough—even when writing draft assignments, be sure to include all sources used to paraphrase, draw ideas, and quote. Put sources into the paper and the bibliography as it is written, not at the end.

5. Use your own words as much as possible—rather than rely on quotes and the words of others, students should "actively engage with the [intellectual] material" rather than stringing together long quotes from other scholars (Harvard Extension School, 2017–2018).

Source: Adapted from Harvard Extension School. (2017–2018). Tips to avoid plagiarism. Harvard University.

The Protection of Human Subjects

Finally, a legal issue confronting researchers is the protection of human subjects. The APA requires researchers to meet certain ethical requirements when using human subjects in research projects. These guidelines include the following:

1. Seeking university approval for the study

2. Getting informed consent from research subjects to participate in the study

3. Obtaining informed consent for recording voices or using images in the study

4. Taking steps to prevent individuals who withdraw or refuse to participate and protecting those that are clients, subordinates, and student participants

5. Only failing to use informed consent when certain factors are met (i.e., data collection is anonymous, where no harm or distress is involved for participants, and where no federal, legal, or institutional regulations exist)

6. Avoiding offering excessive inducements to coerce research participation

7. Avoiding deception in the research, especially if there is the potential for harm or distress for human subjects

8. Providing a debriefing for participants

9. Humanely providing, caring for, and disposing of any animals that participate in research studies (APA, 2018)

Exercise 6.1

You are a student in a criminal justice class. Your professor requires a survey study of 15 undergraduate students on drug use and abuse. Since human subjects will be involved in the study, what steps or procedures should you take to ensure the protection of their rights and welfare? What are your school's IRB requirements?

APA format suggests that authors include descriptions of how they accomplished these guidelines in any papers or presentations resulting from their studies. Additionally, the association suggests that protecting the confidentiality of research participants is the primary responsibility of the researcher. To protect confidentiality, the researcher should avoid "disclosing confidential, personally identifiable information concerning their patients, individual or organizational clients, students, research participants, or other recipients of their services" (APA, 2018). To protect confidentiality, a researcher can allow the participant to read and consent to the written material once the data have been analyzed and summarized and/or the researcher can disguise some aspect of the participant, such as changing their name, altering characteristics, limiting descriptions of characteristics, using composites, or adding extraneous information to the descriptions (APA, 2010, p. 17).

Additional methods of protecting human subjects are provided by educational institutions and government entities that play a part in research that uses human participants. These bodies mandate IRBs that provide for the ethical and regulatory oversight of research projects. IRBs have the ability to approve, make modifications to, and reject research proposals that involve human subject participation. Fundamental in their role is to ensure that human subjects are humanely treated and that their rights and welfare are protected during the study's duration. The IRB reviews research protocol and other materials prior to the beginning of the study and before any humans participate to make their determinations regarding appropriateness. Legal mandates, like those published in the *Federal Register* (2018), require IRB reviews for studies funded by federal agencies. Universities, although not federally mandated to have IRBs unless they participate in federally funded research, usually require students and faculty to seek IRB approval before participating in projects involving human subjects. Not doing so can result in sanctions for the student and/or faculty member and, in the case of funded research, revocation of the funding and termination of the research project. Thus, researchers planning a study using human participants should become familiar with their institution's IRB standards and review procedures.

Exercise 6.2

What would you do if you knew a student in your class was selling papers to other students to submit for grades in a course. Is this an ethical or legal violation? Why or why not? Since you know of the infraction, can you be held accountable if you choose not to do anything?

Typically, the review process is similar across all institutions and includes an application, a review, and a decision. The application asks researchers to identify the research project, hypothesis, methods, and methodology, as well as specific characteristics about the human subjects to be recruited, their participation expectations, harms, duress, rewards, and debriefing procedures. Other questions and documents, like the informed consent forms, may be required with the application and used to determine if the rights and welfare of the subjects are protected (*Federal Register*, 2018). If the researcher is not using protected groups, such as prisoners, pregnant women, children, in vitro fertilization, or mentally incompetent persons, the IRB may choose to use an expedited review process where only one or two members of the board review the application and make a decision. If, however, protected groups are being recruited for the study, a full board review will be required before a decision can be made to approve, modify, or disapprove of the research application (*Federal Register*, 2018). The review process can take several months, so researchers should consider this when preparing to complete a research study.

In summary, research is guided not only by the ethical standards developed by the APA, but also by legal and ethical expectations set by the federal government and educational institutions. Students in criminal justice are expected to know and understand the importance of using a uniform style of writing to present research and to follow the "sound and rigorous standards of scientific communication" (APA, 2010, p. xiii). The APA sets this style and provides a format, or simple set of rules (e.g., style rules), to facilitate reading comprehension in the social and behavioral sciences. Found in the APA *Publication Manual,* the style rules provide a model of writing across many social science disciplines and bring together the diverse approaches and scholarship for the benefit of readers and scientific literature, in general.

Modern Language Association and the Chicago Manual of Style

This chapter would be remiss if two additional styles of writing were not mentioned, albeit briefly. As discussed in detail earlier, the APA format is the most widely accepted style in social and behavioral science writing; however, two other styles of writing are sometimes used in journals, magazines, and at educational institutions. These styles are the MLA and the *CMOS.*

Modern Language Association (MLA)

The MLA was founded in 1883 and is the most frequently used formatting style in the humanities and liberal arts (MLA, 2018). The MLA hosts national conferences and an informative website for style rules and formatting. With more than 25,000 members, the MLA has worked to "strengthen the study and teaching of language and literature" (MLA, 2018, n.p.). Like APA format, the MLA has established writing guidelines for formatting, page layout, abbreviations, footnotes, quotations, citations, and preparing manuscripts for publication. It also includes guidelines for plagiarism. Unlike APA format, which provides very specific style rules for almost every type of source in a lengthy manual, the MLA uses a core elements approach to citing sources. In this approach, writers only need to identify nine elements in each source:

1. Author

2. Title of source

3. Title of container

4. Other contributors

5. Version

6. Number

7. Publisher

8. Publication date

9. Location (MLA, 2018)

Once the writer has identified these core elements, he or she can use this format for basically any type of resource. If the source is a smaller work inside of a larger work (i.e., a poem in a book of poetry), the writer should consider the smaller work (poem) the source, while the larger work (book of poetry) is the container. The container is identified in the core elements as is the smaller work. Those interested in MLA style format can visit the MLA website at www.mla.org for more information.

Chicago Manual of Style (CMOS)

Last, but certainly not least, is *CMOS*. This style of writing is normally used in history and a few social sciences. This style uses two formats when citing resources. The first is the notes and bibliography system, which relies on footnotes and endnotes to create references to sources used in papers. In this system, the quote or paraphrase is numbered, and the corresponding number is placed at the end of the page or within a list of references with the full information needed to locate the source. The second system is an author–date system, where the author's name is found first in a reference and the date is placed last in the reference. More information on the systems used by *CMOS* can be found in the manual or online at www.chicagomanual ofstyle.org/home.html.

The main differences in the three styles of writing—APA, MLA, and the *CMOS*—is where the emphasis is placed on citing sources and references and which disciplines use the style. APA format is most commonly used in the social sciences and places emphasis on the date the work was created. The date of publication is placed in in-text citations immediately following the quote or paraphrase and immediately after the author's name in the references. The most recent style rules for APA format can be found in the newest edition of the *APA Publication Manual* on the APA website at www.apastyle .org and on the Purdue OWL: APA Formatting and Style Guide at https://owl.purdue.edu/owl/research_and_citation/apa_style/apa_for-matting_and_style_guide/general_format.html. MLA is primarily used in the humanities and liberal arts and emphasizes the authorship of the work. The author's name is placed in in-text citations in the body of the paper, and the author's name is found first in the references section of the paper. MLA uses core elements to format citations that apply to almost any type of source. The formatting can be found in the newest edition of the MLA manual. Last, *CMOS* is used by some social sciences, but mostly in history. The *CMOS* uses two types of citation and reference styles: a notes and bibliography system and an author–date system. The notes style is generally used by history and relies on footnotes and endnotes when citing sources. The *CMOS* latest guidelines can be found in the manual. Even though there are multiple formats of writing, students in criminal justice use APA formatting and follow the ethical and legal standards put forth by the APA *Publication Manual*, universities, and federal mandates.

CHAPTER SUMMARY

Regardless of the writing system used, formatting and writing style are important to simplify the writing process for the author and to make things easier for the reader. By following standard guidelines in writing, authors within disciplines can more easily create and publish works for general consumption and for use in academic scholarship. The rules in which they design their research are agreed upon by all within the discipline so researchers can focus on the essence of the research. Thanks to style rules, readers can effortlessly identify sources within written documents and can read for understanding rather than worrying about the style rules of grammar, citation, referencing, graphing, etc. In the social sciences, particularly, criminal justice, the APA sets the style rules followed by researchers, writers, and publishers.

In addition to general style rules, the APA provides guiding principles in research and writing ethics. Federal government offices provide legal mandates on research, and universities comply with both the ethical and legal standards by reviewing and ensuring that students and faculty are following the laws, protecting human subjects, and providing credit for works used in their investigations. Individuals found to violate the ethical or legal directives may find that they experience civil or criminal penalties and/or are ruined as writers, authors, or researchers.

QUESTIONS FOR CONSIDERATION

1. Identify the most pressing ethical issue in social science research, in your opinion.
2. What is the definition of plagiarism? What is the difference between plagiarism and self-plagiarism?
3. Why is it important to protect human subjects involved in academic research?
4. Identify an ethical violation commonly committed by students at a university. Why is this behavior unethical?

The Academic Research Paper

Many students cringe at the very thought of writing a research paper. It is often viewed both by strong writers and those who lack confidence in their writing skills as a tedious, boring assignment that requires a great deal of time to complete. This chapter will introduce students to conducting research, locating and evaluating sources, reading scholarly journal articles, and writing a research paper using credible sources. The Appendix also includes a sample student essay. With the guidance contained in this chapter, students should no longer dread a research paper assignment.

The Research Writing Process

The research paper is similar to other kinds of essays, "the difference being the use of documented source material to support, illustrate, or explain" the writer's ideas (Wyrick, 2013, p. 371). It is "a documented essay containing citations to the source you have consulted (that) combines your own ideas, experiences, and attitudes with supporting information provided by other sources" (Schiffhorst & Schell, 1991, p. 325). Readers may also find your resources useful to their research of similar topics.

Create a Realistic Schedule

Writing well takes time, so plan your time well. Always begin by setting a realistic schedule for completing the essay, taking account for the responsibilities and activities in one's life such as other classes and assignments, home life, work, and social time. Consult the course syllabus and review the course policies for submitting assignments. Many professors will not accept late submissions or will significantly lower the grade for late work. It is always safest to treat the assignment due date as an absolute deadline with no option for submitting the paper late.

Students will usually have several weeks to complete an essay assignment, but should not fall into the procrastination trap by putting things off that are not immediately due. Start planning and brainstorming topic ideas as soon as the assignment is received. Allow time for brainstorming, researching, drafting, and revising, revising, revising, and pay close attention to drafts or other assignments due before the research essay's final due date.

Finally, print or create a paper copy of the schedule and post it in a conspicuous place to serve as a constant reminder. A sample schedule based on a five-page research essay is shown in Table 7.1.

Table 7.1 Sample Paper-Planning Schedule

Task	Required Time	Due Date
Research essay assignment received from professor on		Assigned on Aug. 20
Brainstorm topic ideas	1 hour	
Quick Internet search to ensure source material is readily available	1 hour	
Research	3 hours (minimum—more for longer assignments)	
Writing, Rough Draft 1	5 hours	
Submit Draft 1		**Due Sept. 3**
Writing, Rough Draft 2	3 hours	
Submit Draft 2		**Due Sept. 10**
Research	2 hours	
Writing, Create References page	1 hour	
Writing, Final Draft and editing	3 hours	
Submit Final Research Essay		**Due Sept. 16**
Total time based on a five-page essay	19 hours	

Select a Topic

A professor may assign the research essay topic, or a student may be free to select a topic. One way to make the research essay assignment more satisfying for the writer and interesting for the reader is to write about a familiar topic. "The best way to avoid . . . needless drudgery is to choose a subject you already know something about and want to learn more about" (Schiffhorst & Schell, 1991, p. 327). Consider choosing "something that interests you. You'll be spending a lot of time on this assignment, and you'll be happier writing about a topic that engages you" (Brown, 2014, p. 244). Take the time to fully explore the choices, making certain the topic satisfies the requirements of the assignment. It is always best to check with the professor for additional insight and final approval.

Focus on the Topic

Inexperienced writers often choose an essay topic that lacks focus. If a student were to research police body cameras, for example, it would be impossible to read and evaluate the information contained in the thousands of websites, journal articles, and databases that would be discovered.

Before beginning the research, one should develop some specific ideas on what the audience should know about the topic. An essay on police body cameras might focus on one of the following more narrow concepts:

1. Do police body cameras reduce use of excessive force incidents?

2. What is the effect of body cameras on community relations?

3. Can the use of body cameras reduce the number of misconduct complaints?

4. Is a citizen's right to privacy violated by the use of body cameras?

5. Can the use of body cameras increase the safety of officers and the public?

When considering a topic, a writer should make certain a sufficient body of literature exists to support the thesis. While an abundance of information about police body cameras can be easily located, little has been written about police accreditation. Despite its interest to the writer, choosing a topic without easily available and adequate resources will make researching and writing the research paper especially difficult.

Conducting Research

Primary and Secondary Sources

Primary sources include research, publications, reports, interviews, and other original material (Schiffhorst & Schell, 1991). Secondary sources are created with the support of primary sources. Primary sources give a truer sense of the topic than any secondary source could provide (Bombaro, 2012). Collecting data for a primary source, though, can be challenging. Obtaining primary source data requires conducting individual or focus group interviews, completing survey research, or observing participant behavior, and the process can be both costly and time-consuming. Some primary source data collected by researchers are available on criminal justice databases. For example, a student researching family violence might consult a Bureau of Justice Statistics (BJS) report. The report is a primary source since it is based on crime statistics collected and analyzed by the BJS, and this information is essential to understanding the issue. Students should "locate and use as many primary sources as possible" (Schiffhorst & Schell, 1991, p. 336).

Exercise 7.1

Each of the topic questions listed below is too broad for a research essay assignment. For each, list two or three ideas on how these topics could be focused into a more appropriate essay topic.

1. Do police officers use too much force?

2. Does segregation really protect inmates from violence?

3. Should all juveniles who commit a felony be charged as an adult?

4. What challenges does a felon face when seeking employment?

Secondary sources rely on interpreting primary or other secondary sources to support or counter the author's thesis. These include books, scholarly articles, and other documents authored by someone who did not conduct original research or experience the event first-hand (Brown, 2014). Students should evaluate secondary sources carefully for credibility. Companies and organizations often fund research with the intent of a predetermined outcome. Information about evaluating sources is included later in this chapter.

Locating Sources

General Search Engines

The Internet is an important resource and should be a part of the research plan. With just a few keystrokes, a seemingly endless collection of information can be located. Google, Bing, and Ask are the most popular general search engines, but students should always be cautious of Internet information since anyone can post information to the Web (Ratcliff, 2018).

Search engines seek matches to search terms by scanning millions of Web pages (Hacker, 2006). General search engines can be a good starting point for research, and even Wikipedia can identify valuable source information. But general search engines should not be used as a primary source for information. Later in this chapter, we discuss evaluating the credibility of sources.

Use Search Parameters

Writers should use search parameters to refine and focus a search.

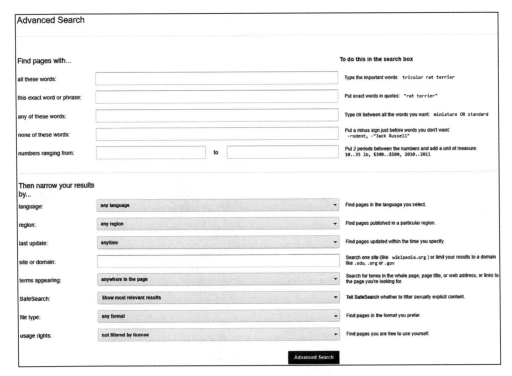

Source: Google and the Google logo are registered trademarks of Google LLC. Used with permission.

1. Use quotation marks around words to search for an exact phrase: "police use of force."

2. Put – in front of words that should not appear in the results: police – sheriff.

3. Use OR if either of two terms should appear in the results: police or sheriff.

4. Insert "site:" in front of a word to search for websites or domains: Site: corrections.

Many search engines have an Advanced Search page for other search options, as shown by the Google example on the previous page.

Google Scholar

Google Scholar (GS) can help focus a search since it omits general readership returns. Google describes the site as "a simple way to broadly search for scholarly literature . . . (such as) articles, theses, books, abstracts and court opinions, from academic publishers, professional societies, online repositories, universities and other web sites" (Google Scholar, n.d.). Anyone who knows how to use Google can effectively use GS to quickly access research articles completed by scholarly authors. Like any product, though, GS is not without criticism. Shultz (2007) suggests the advanced search function can be unreliable and that some returns may not be scholarly. Like any source, GS should be used cautiously by the researcher, and materials should be evaluated critically. GS should never be the sole source of identifying research materials, and it should never replace library databases. Nevertheless, GS can be an effective starting point for students to identify scholarly materials and authors. Cathcart and Roberts (2006) suggest GS is but one database and is best used "as a bridge to the more reliable, comprehensive resources offered by the libraries" (p. 14).

Use Country Codes

According to Alan November (2016), the challenge of Internet research is in "learning how to access and synthesize massive amounts of information from all over the world. To manage overwhelming amounts of information, it is critical to learn how to design searches that take you past the first page of results" (para. 8).

Google's default setting is to search websites in the region where the search originates. Whenever a student researches a problem that involves another country, he and she should use a country code to generate sources from that country (November, 2016). For example, perhaps a student wants to research differences in police use of force between the United States and the United Kingdom. Using the search terms "use of force" and "differences in US and UK policy" returns few results. But adding the search term "site:" and the country code UK (site: uk) focuses the search to UK sources and provides insightful information that might not otherwise be found. Adding "ac" to the search term, such as site: ac.uk, limits results to UK academic institutions. A list of country codes can be found at www.web-l.com/country-codes/.

Exercise 7.2

1. What name do the British use for the American Revolutionary War?
   Search: site: uk American Revolutionary War

2. What was the Russian name for the war on the eastern front in WWII?
   Search: site: ru wwII eastern front

3. How is gun ownership reported by United Kingdom and American news outlets?
   Search: site: uk US gun ownership, site: us gun ownership

See answers on p. 108.

Use Databases

Criminal Justice Databases

Criminal Justice databases focus on issues related to crime, prisons and jails, probation and parole, juvenile justice, and the courts. The information located in these databases comes from journals, books, and government reports. Use these and other related databases when researching a criminal justice topic.

1. National Criminal Justice Reference Service: www.ncjrs.gov/index.html

2. National Archive of Criminal Justice Data: www.icpsr.umich.edu/icpsrweb/content/NACJD/index.html

3. Bureau of Justice Statistics: www.bjs.gov/

4. Federal Bureau of Investigations Publications: https://ucr.fbi.gov/ucr-publications

5. Criminal Justice Abstracts (Access through an institution or local library. See Library Databases)

6. Journal Storage (JSTOR): www.jstor.org/

Students can find an extensive listing of criminal justice databases compiled by the University of Michigan at http://libguides.umflint.edu/c.php?g=428962&p=3263967.

Library Databases

Some databases charge a subscription fee and are not as straightforward to access as general search engines. Most college libraries and some public libraries subscribe to databases that provide unlimited access to scholarly resources not available on the Internet (Hacker, 2006). Databases like ProQuest, EBSCOhost, and LexisNexis fall into this category. Check the library website or ask a librarian about how to access these sites.

Source: Abraham Baldwin Agricultural College Libraries. http://www.abac.edu/academics/bald win-library.

LexisNexis Academic

The LexisNexis database contains information collected from thousands of legal and news sources. Full-text publications are available from newspapers, legal news, magazines, medical journals, trade publications, transcripts, wire service reports, government publications, law reviews, and reference works (LexisNexis Academic, n.d.). LexisNexis Academic is available only by subscription.

ProCon.org

ProCon.org describes itself as a "nonprofit nonpartisan public charity (that) provides professionally researched pro, con, and related information on more than 50 controversial issues . . . by presenting controversial issues in a straightforward, nonpartisan, and primarily pro-con format" (ProCon, 2018). Students who struggle with selecting a topic will find the site's broad selection of timely and relevant issues to be an excellent starting point for the research paper.

Topics are introduced with a thorough summary followed by an easy-to-read, side-by-side debate of both sides of the issue. The site notes, for example, that police body cameras may improve officer accountability, while acknowledging the cameras may invade the privacy of citizens (ProCon, 2018). Source information is well-documented, and facts can be evaluated for accuracy.

Traditional News Sources

Although print and traditional TV news outlets have faded in popularity, newspapers and network channel news sources remain valuable sources of information for researchers. EBSCO, a leading provider of databases and information sources to libraries, provides access to full-text newspapers covering national and international events (EBSCO, 2018). Transcripts from television and radio news casts are also available. Many college and university libraries subscribe to EBSCO*host*, where students can access "nearly 60 full-text national and international newspapers and more than 320 full-text regional newspapers" (EBSCO, 2018, para. 3).

Benefit From Previous Research in the Topic Area

Students can benefit from the work of authors who have studied and published research similar to their topic. When a source is located, students should carefully read the reference page, paying particular attention to titles that appear to be closely related to their topic. The bibliographic information should be added to the Working Bibliography. Using the author's name and title of the work, search one of the earlier described databases until the source is located. It is always best to locate a full-text copy of the source. Students can read the full details of the work and evaluate its usefulness to their research essay.

Evaluating Sources

All source material should be evaluated thoroughly, since anyone can post information to the Web. Using a questionable source can discredit an essay and the writer. According to Kirszner and Mandell (2011), students should ask four questions when evaluating sources:

1. Is the source *respected*? Peer-reviewed scholarly articles are valued much more than general readership articles. Likewise, a major news publication, like the *Wall Street Journal* or the *New York Times*, is considered a more dependable source than an independent newspaper.

2. Is the source *reliable*? Reliable sources depend on factual, documented information that supports the thesis. In a reliable source, the author will include source citations that can be checked for accuracy.

3. Is the source *current*? Current sources provide information relevant to the topic. There is no standard for how old a publication might be yet still remain current. A technology article could be outdated in a year or less, while information on Community Policing from the 1980s might be current.

4. Is the author of the source *credible*? What other publications has the author written, and has he or she been cited by other researchers? Is the author employed by company or foundation that suggests a particular bias? (pp. 760–761)

The use of credible sources is a sign of a well-written essay.

How to Read a Scholarly Article

Critically reading a scholarly article can be challenging for students. Even for students who are strong readers, the scholarly article is unique from other writing genres. The format, language, and data tables make it an "active, complex process of making meaning in which a reader draws information from several sources and concurrently constructs a representation of a text's message" (McLoughlin, 1995, p. 29).

Scholarly articles follow a specific format that includes an Abstract, Introduction, Literature Review, Research Methods, Analysis, Findings or Results, Discussion, and References. The Abstract appears at the beginning of the article and is usually limited to about 250 words. It is a summary of the problem examined by the author, an overview of the study, and the author's findings. The Introduction identifies the need for research in the topic area, identifies the focus of the study, and its relevance to the field, such as criminology. To fully understand the issue, a Literature Review is included, which is the author's research in the topic area. The Literature Review is described in more detail later in this chapter. The Research Methods section includes information about critical aspects of the study: the data, the research sample, and a description of the statistical or other methods used to analyze the data. First, it is important to understand the source of the type of data to be analyzed. Are the data qualitative or quantitative? Quantitative data are numbers, while qualitative data are text, such as subject interviews and observations of study subjects. Is the author using primary or secondary data, and how were the data collected? Next, it is critical to understand the unit of analysis. In other words, what exactly is the researcher analyzing: individual people, groups, criminal justice agencies or programs, or other outcome measures? Virtually anything can be analyzed. Finally, what methods did the author use in the analysis? The Analysis section is often the most difficult for students to comprehend. In this section, the researcher reports in detail the application of statistical methods or other means of data analysis and the outcomes of the data analysis. Charts, graphs, and other visual representation of the analysis are included in this section. In the Findings or Results section, the author interprets the results of the data analysis. In this section, the researcher applies the outcome of the analysis to the research questions and determines if the analysis supports or refutes those questions. Finally, the author summarizes the study in the Discussion section. Researchers often discuss the limitations of the study, if the findings add to the scientific literature in the field, and the need for future studies in similar areas not included in the study.

Successful students often employ a strategy when reading scholarly articles rather than using an approach similar to other reading assignments. If an English professor assigns Nathaniel Hawthorne's *The Scarlet Letter*, the most efficient approach to reading the text is to start at the beginning and continue straight through to the end. But this approach is often not the most effective way to read a scholarly article. Students should first read the Title, Abstract, and Discussion. This will help the student determine the nature of the study, what the author intended to prove, and if the study was successful toward that end. Next, skim the Literature Review, Research Methods, and Analysis to understand how the study was conducted. Then reread the Results and Discussion sections closely. Students should then scan the References section to identify other studies that may benefit their research. Lastly, students should make brief notes or annotations while reading the scholarly article with a particular focus on areas that might be useful to their research.

Not every published article is written well, and it is highly unlikely that every study discovered and read by a student will be valuable to the research at hand. With some practice, though, this reading strategy will help students understand the scholarly article and decide if it can add value to their study.

Writing a Literature Review

Scholarly articles and essays written for graduate-level criminal justice courses require the inclusion of a literature review. Professors who teach undergraduate courses may require a literature review as well. The literature review is a summary of what the literature says about a specific topic (Purdue OWL, 2018d). It is essential for a writer to understand the topic, theoretical perspectives, problems in researching the topic, and major controversies in the topic area of any research project (Adams, Kahn, Raeside, & White, 2007). Reading as much of the available literature as possible is the only way to do this.

The abundance of literature in any topic area requires students to narrow the topic and focus the research questions so that identified literature in the topic area is itself as limited and focused as possible. That said, a search in most topic areas will return an abundance of potential sources. Reading source material will increase the student's knowledge in the topic area and lead to other potential source material. When reading, students should identify experts in the field and seek out their literature in the topic area. Reading will also reveal theoretical perspectives used to identify the type of data needed to answer the research questions (Adams et al., 2007). Additionally, problems with researching the topic area may be identified when reading the literature. For example, Jacobs (1999) observed that no official data exist on criminal offenses committed by police officers. With this knowledge derived from the literature, scholars interested in researching this topic understand that locating data will be problematic to their study.

The literature review is a critical piece of a research project. Reading the available literature will improve the student's knowledge of the topic and may allow him or her to speak to topic experts. Perhaps most rewarding, though, is the feeling of inclusion derived from the connection between other scholars' work and the writer's. As noted by Adams et al. (2007), writing the literature review introduces students to an academic community as someone "who can speak and write with confidence and authority on a specific research problem" (p. 39).

Writing the Essay

Presenting the information contained in a research essay in a clear and ordered fashion is essential to the essay's effectiveness. Students may find creating an outline of the essay's major points helpful in organizing the logical flow of ideas. Follow the outline, but do not be afraid to move information if it fits better elsewhere (Kirszner & Mandell, 2011). Every essay should be structured logically with a distinct introduction, body, and conclusion.

The introduction section is usually one paragraph in length, but it may be several paragraphs for longer assignments. The thesis statement is often the last sentence in this paragraph. It is a clearly written, single sentence intended to inform the reader of the writer's main idea.

Body paragraphs support the thesis statement. The writer's ideas are supported by paraphrases and quotations from sources and the writer's opinion (Kirszner & Mandell, 2011). Each paragraph should begin with a clear topic sentence using language identical or similar to the thesis statement and focus on a single idea. The last sentence of each body paragraph should be a transition sentence. This sentence signals the reader that the topic is about to change.

Finally, the conclusion paragraph summarizes the essay. It should include a sentence that restates the thesis statement as a reminder of the writer's main idea. The conclusion should be at least one paragraph, but it may be longer if needed.

Working and Annotated Bibliographies

A working bibliography is a list of sources consulted (Hacker, 2006). The working bibliography is the beginnings of the references page that appears on the last page of the research essay and can be reviewed to relocate source material during the writing process (see Figure 7.1 for an example of a references list). Researchers often locate many more sources than they actually use, so not all sources identified in a working bibliography will appear on the references page (Hacker, 2006).

The Internet makes creating a working bibliography a relatively simple process. All that is necessary is to capture the author's name, the title of the source, and the URL or reference site where the source was originally located. For example, a student researching the effect of prison architecture on inmate behavior on GS might locate a journal article titled "Prison Architecture and Inmate Misconduct: A Multilevel Assessment." This information can then be copied and pasted into a Working Bibliography Word document and saved for later reference.

Prison architecture and inmate misconduct: A multilevel assessment   [PDF] researchgate.net

RG Morris, JL Worrall - Crime & Delinquency, 2014 - journals.sagepub.com
Researchers have not yet devoted sufficient attention to the effect of **prison architecture** on inmate misconduct. Using data from the population of male prisoners in Texas, the authors explored the association between two **prison** architectural design types (as determined by …
☆ ⁹⁹ Cited by 72   Related articles   All 8 versions

Source: Google and the Google logo are registered trademarks of Google LLC. Used with permission.

Clicking the quotation mark at the bottom of the source opens a new window containing the complete source information formatted in several reference styles. The APA format for this article is displayed below.

Morris, R. G., & Worrall, J. L. (2014). Prison architecture and inmate misconduct: A multilevel assessment. *Crime & Delinquency, 60*(7), 1083–1109.

The annotated bibliography includes more detail than the working bibliography. An annotated bibliography includes the bibliographic details as well as a brief summary of the source content (Wyrick, 2013). The annotated bibliography serves several important purposes. For the student writer, "it demonstrates that you've read your sources and understand them, and it serves as practice for 'real' research" (Brown, 2014, p. 240). For other researchers, an annotated bibliography is a valuable resource. If an annotated bibliography is available in the researcher's topic area, time and effort can be saved in locating source information.

Exercise 7.3

1. Enter this URL into a Web browser to access an annotated bibliography on women offenders prepared by the National Institute of Corrections Information Center: http://static.nicic.gov.s3 .amazonaws.com/Library/021385.pdf.

2. Refer to the search parameters mentioned earlier in this chapter. Use a search parameter to locate an annotated bibliography on teen dating violence.

CHAPTER SUMMARY

This chapter introduced students to writing an academic essay using credible sources. Writing a successful essay begins with understanding the assignment due dates, including those before the final essay is submitted. Creating a writing schedule can help students meet these deadlines. Students should select a topic and focus the research questions to a topic area in which a sufficient body of literature exists to support the thesis. Literature can be found using primary and secondary sources identified through the Internet, library resources, criminal justice databases, and news sources. Students must critically analyze these sources for its respect as a scholarly source, as well as its reliability, currency, and credibility. By following the guidance contained in this chapter, students should find writing an academic essay a rewarding and educational experience.

ADDITIONAL READING

1. "Writing a Research Paper." Available at https://owl.english.purdue.edu/owl/resource/658/01/.

2. "Writing a Research Paper." Available at https://writing.wisc.edu/Handbook/PlanResearchPaper.html.

QUESTIONS FOR CONSIDERATION

1. The research essay is similar to other types of essays. What is a major difference between the research essay and other essays?

2. List and describe the four questions a student should ask when evaluating sources.

3. Define primary source and secondary source. Include a discussion of the advantages and disadvantages of each.

4. Discuss the advantages of using country codes for a search.

5. Visit a criminal justice database. Describe the information that can be found on the site and discuss how this information can benefit your research.

EXERCISE ANSWERS

Exercise 6.2 Answers

1. The American War for Independence

2. The Great Patriotic War

3. First page results for UK sites focus on gun control, while US results focus on gun ownership.

Appendix A
EBSCOhost Law and Political Science Database Search Results

....

1. An Officer's Eyes and Ears, Recording All. By: Manjoo, Farhad. New York Times. 8/21/2014, Vol. 163 Issue 56600, pB1-B8. 377-391.
2. Balance Privacy With Public Good. By: Smith, Chris. USA Today. 05/07/2015.
3. Body Camera Video Release Is Halted, Temporarily. By: Southall, Ashley. New York Times. 5/15/2018, Vol. 167 Issue 57963.
4. Body Cameras and the Path to Redeem Privacy Law. By: Hartzog, Woodrow. North Carolina Law Review. 2018, Vol. 96 Issue 5, p1257-1312.
5. Body of Evidence Grows, But Questions Remain About Police Body Cameras. By: Ebi, Kevin. American City & County Exclusive Insight. 9/28/2016, p1-1. 1p.
6. Body-Mounted Police Cameras: A Primer on Police Accountability vs. Privacy. By: Simmons, Kami Chavis. Howard Law Journal. Spring2015, Vol. 58 Issue 3, p881-890.
7. Body-Worn Cameras for Police Accountability: Opportunities and Risks. By: Coudert, Fanny; Butin, Denis; Le Métayer, Daniel. Computer Law & Security Review. Dec2015, Vol. 31 Issue 6, p749-762.
8. Cameras on Cops a Privacy Question. By: Madhani, Aamer; USA Today. 05/06/2015.
9. Can Cameras Stop the Killings? Racial Differences in Perceptions of the Effectiveness of Body-Worn Cameras in Police Encounters. By: Ray, Rashawn; Marsh, Kris; Powelson, Connor. Sociological Forum. Dec2017, Supplement S1, Vol. 32, p1032-1050.
10. Collateral Visibility: A Socio-Legal Study of Police Body-Camera Adoption, Privacy, and Public Disclosure in Washington State. By: Newell, Bryce Clayton. Indiana Law Journal. Fall2017, Vol. 92 Issue 4, p1329-1399, 71p, 5 Charts, 7 Graphs, Database: Legal Source.
11. Fourth Amendment Implications of Police-Worn Body Cameras. By: Nielsen, Erik. St. Mary's Law Journal. 2016, Vol. 48 Issue 1, p115-143.
12. Implementing a Body-Worn Camera. By: Miller, Lindsay; Toliver, Jessica, Corporate Author: Police Executive Research Forum (PERF). 2014.
13. In the Eyes of the Law: The Effects of Body-Worn Cameras on Police Behavior, Citizen Interactions, and Privacy. By: Heumann, Milton; Kavin, Rick; Chugh, Anu; Cassak, Lance. Criminal Law Bulletin. May/Jun2018, Vol. 54 Issue 3, p584-627.
14. Oklahoma City Police, Union Reach Agreement on Body Cameras. By: Dean, Joel. Journal Record Legislative Report (Oklahoma City, OK). 11/29/2016.
15. Open City. By: Funk, Mckenzie. New York Times Magazine. 10/23/2016, p31-51.
16. Out of Focus: Zooming in on Body Cameras, Privacy, and Medical Emergencies. By: Arrabito, James S. Rutgers University Law Review. Winter2017, Vol. 69 Issue 2, p741-789.
17. Panel Ponders Stricter Law on Release of Police Body Camera Videos. By: Stephenson, Hank. Arizona Capitol Times (Phoenix, AZ). 11/25/2015.

18. Past the Pilot Stage: Policy Makers Must Consider Impacts of Police Body-Worn Cameras Beyond Accountability. By: Miller, Katie. Harvard Kennedy School Review. 2019, Vol. 19, p148-153.
19. Police Body Camera Footage: It's Just Evidence. By: Synan, Bridget M. Duquesne Law Review. Summer2019, Vol. 57 Issue 2, p351-381.
20. Police Body Cams. By: Williams, Rich. State Legislatures. Dec2015, Vol. 41 Issue 10, p16-17.
21. Police Body-Worn Camera Footage: A Question of Access. By: Pagliarella, Chris. Yale Law & Policy Review. Spring2016, Vol. 34 Issue 2, p533-543.
22. Police Body-Worn Cameras. By: Stoughton, Seth W. North Carolina Law Review. 2018, Vol. 96 Issue 5, p1363-1424.
23. Police Cam Downside: Your Arrest Hits YouTube. By: Williams, Timothy. New York Times. 4/27/2015, Vol. 164 Issue 56849, pA1-A13.
24. Police-Worn Body Cameras: Balancing Privacy and Accountability Through State and Police Department Action. By: Kampfe, Karson. Ohio State Law Journal. 2015, Vol. 76 Issue 5, p1153-1200.
25. Privacy and Cybersecurity Lessons at the Intersection of the Internet of Things and Police Body-Worn Cameras. By: Swire, Peter; Woo, Jesse. North Carolina Law Review. 2018, Vol. 96 Issue 5, p1475-1524.
26. Privacy, Public Disclosure, Police Body Cameras: Policy Splits. By: Fan, Mary D. Alabama Law Review. 2016, Vol. 68 Issue 2, p396-444.
27. Recording a New Frontier in Evidence-Gathering: Police Body-Worn Cameras and Privacy Doctrines in Washington State. By: Farden, Katie. Seattle University Law Review. 2016, Vol. 40 Issue 1, p271-298.
28. Resources on Body-Worn Cameras. By: Coppola, Michele. Edited By: Coppola, Michele. TECHBeat, National Law Enforcement and Corrections Technology Center. Jul/Aug2015.
29. Slow Your Roll Out of Body-Worn Cameras: Privacy Concerns and the Tension Between Transparency and Surveillance in Arizona. By: Zwart, Wouter. Arizona Law Review. 2018, Vol. 60 Issue 3, p783-814.
30. Smile, You're on Body Cam. New Scientist. 10/21/2017, Vol. 236 Issue 3148, p3-3.
31. The Lost Language of Privacy. By: Brooks, David. New York Times. 4/14/2015, Vol. 164 Issue 56836, pA23-A23.
32. The Mirage of Use Restrictions. By: Simmons, Ric. North Carolina Law Review. Dec2017, Vol. 96 Issue 1, p133-199.
33. Today's Police Put on a Gun and a Camera. By: Johnson, Kirk. New York Times. 9/28/2014, Vol. 164 Issue 56638, p1-24. 2p.
34. Visibility Is a Trap: The Ethics of Police Body-Worn Cameras and Control. By: Adams, Ian; Mastracci, Sharon. Administrative Theory & Praxis (M. E. Sharpe). Dec2017, Vol. 39 Issue 4, p313-328.
35. Walls Have Eyes. Economist. 6/2/2018, Vol. 427 Issue 9094, Special Section p4-6.
36. What You Need to Know About Body-Worn Cameras: A Primer. By: Bolton, Ben. SceneDoc, Dec2014.
37. When Cameras Are Rolling: Privacy Implications of Body-Mounted Cameras on Police. By: Freund, K. Columbia Journal of Law & Social Problems. Fall2015, Vol. 49 Issue 1, p91-133.
38. Where Is the Goal Line? A Critical Look at Police Body-Worn Camera Programs. By: Alpert, Geoffrey P.; McLean, Kyle. Criminology & Public Policy. Aug2018, Vol. 17 Issue 3, p679-688.

Appendix B
Sample Student Essay

Domestic Violence in Police Families

Student Name

College/University Name

Introduction

The vast majority of police officers go about the business of their profession in a proficient and honorable manner. Each year, millions of people who have contact with the police overwhelmingly report that officers acted properly and were respectful (see the Bureau of Justice Statistics series "Contacts between the police and public," 1999–2008). Every profession, however, has rogue actors.

Despite a vibrant body of literature exploring police misconduct, few studies of crimes committed by police officers exist. Most are limited by a dearth of data or focus upon the actions of officers within a single department. Jacobs (1999) lamented that despite significant resources invested in the police and measuring crime, no official data on criminal acts committed by officers exists, leaving scholars, policymakers, and the public data deprived. The lack of data leaves scholars struggling to understand police criminality (Chappell & Piquero, 2004; Dunn & Caceres, 2010; Eitle, D'Alessio, & Stolzenberg, 2014), but the media are at no loss for dramatic accounts of officer misconduct. A simple Google News search for "police officer arrested" returns over 700,000 news reports, which may lead readers to conclude that crime committed by officers is pervasive and erode the public trust. Sounding official, the CATO Institute maintains the National Police Misconduct Reporting Project (see www.policemisconduct.net/), but it, too, is based on local news reports. Absent credible data, even scholars have turned to the news in search of information on officers involved in criminal acts.

Domestic Violence Committed by Police Officers

Few studies of domestic crime committed by police officers exist, but those that do suggest the frequency of domestic violence is at least as high as or higher among police families than the general population (IACP, 2003; Truman & Morgan, 2014). One study claims that 40 percent of police families experience domestic violence (Neidig, Russell, & Seng, 1992, p. 30), a rate more than twice that experienced in the general population (Truman & Morgan, 2014, p. 1). Another study suggests that in departments serving populations of over 100,000, 55 percent of agencies had a policy directed at handling domestic violence calls involving police officers (as cited in Erwin, Gershon, Tiburzi, & Lin, 2005, p. 14) suggesting police administrators recognize a problem exists.

Explaining Domestic Violence in Police Families

Several studies attempt to identify officer-level attributes that may contribute to domestic violence. One study identified demographics for those officers involved in domestic violence cases in a large, urban department. The majority of officers were minority male patrol officers with a mean age of 34 years. These officers had worked in policing for about 8 years and were typically assigned to high-crime areas (Erwin et al., 2005, p. 15). Additionally, the authors found that most complaints (48 percent) were filed against the officer by the officer's wife followed by the officer's ex-wife or ex-girlfriend (27 percent) and their present girlfriend (22 percent). Most complaints alleged simple battery (77 percent), and a number of officers had a history of at least one previous complaint of domestic violence (23 percent) (Erwin et al., 2005, p. 17). Of the study group members, most were either immediately suspended (64 percent) or arrested (26 percent). Just 8 percent of these cases, though, resulted in any final formal action due to a lack of support from the victim (61 percent) or a lack of evidence (31 percent) (Erwin et al., Lin, 2005, p. 17).

The Impact of Officer Malpractice

Several studies suggest the media play a role in shaping public opinion. The great bulk of police work is isolated from the public's view, and much of what the public knows about the police is derived from the media (Dowler, 2003, p. 112). Repeated exposure to numerous media accounts of misconduct may lead viewers to believe the behavior is rampant (Weitzer & Tuch, 2004, pp. 308–309) and is strongly correlated with citizen perception of police conduct (Weitzer & Tuch, 2004, p. 321). Chermak, McGarrell, and Gruenewald (2006) found the more a person read news accounts of officer misconduct, the more likely they felt the officer was guilty (p. 272).

Responses to Domestic Violence by Police Officers

Perhaps most instrumental in revealing the problem of domestic violence acts committed by police officers was the federal Omnibus Consolidated Appropriations Act of 1996, otherwise known as the Lautenberg Amendment. The Amendment altered the Gun Control Act of 1968, which was designed to prevent the use of guns in domestic violence situations (Halstead, 2001, p. 2). Its most significant effect on police officers is that it removed the "public service" exemption, which previously allowed local, state, and federal officers to continue to carry and use firearms for employment-related duties (Halstead, 2001, p. 2). This retroactive act, though, made it illegal for anyone convicted of a domestic violence crime involving physical violence or a firearm, including police officers, from owning or using a firearm (Johnson, Todd, & Subramanian, 2005, p. 3). This legislation forced agencies that may have previously ignored or informally addressed domestic violence within their ranks to identify past offenders and review and update agency policies on handling cases when the suspect is an officer (Johnson et al., 2005, p. 3).

Conclusion

The purpose of this Appendix was to survey the available literature in an effort to better understand what is known about domestic violence in police families, its predictors, and the criminal justice system response to events when they occur. While few studies exist that examine domestic violence that occurs in police families, a number of studies suggest the rate of domestic violence committed by police officers may be higher than that of the general population.

While no profession is without its rogue actors, officers who commit acts of domestic violence must be dealt with swiftly in order to protect victims and the public trust. Successful policing is based on a relationship of trust between the police and the community they serve, for "(w)ithout trust between police and citizens, effective policing is impossible" (United States Department of Justice, 1994, p. vii).

Figure 6.1   Example Reference List

References

Adams, J., Raeside, R., & Khan, H. A. (2014). *Research Methods for Business and Social Science Students.* New Delhi, India: Sage Publications Pvt. Ltd.

Barnett, O. W., Miller-Perrin, C. L., & Perrin, R. D. (2011). *Family violence across the lifespan: An introduction.* Thousand Oaks, CA: Sage.

Blackwell, B. S., & Vaughn, M. S. (2003). Police civil liability for inappropriate response to domestic assault victims. *Journal of Criminal Justice, 31*(2), 129–146.

Castle Rock v. Gonzales, 545 U.S. 04-278 (2005).

Çelik, A. (2013). An analysis of mandatory arrest policy on domestic violence. *International Journal of Human Sciences, 10*(1), 1503–1523.

Chappell, A. T., & Piquero, A. R. (2004). Applying social learning theory to police misconduct. *Deviant Behavior, 25*(2), 89–108.

Chermak, S., McGarrell, E., & Gruenewald, J. (2006). Media coverage of police misconduct and attitudes toward police. *Policing, 29*(2), 261–281.

Dowler, K. (2003). Media consumption and public attitudes toward crime and justice: The relationship between fear of crime, punitive attitudes, and perceived police effectiveness. *Journal of Criminal Justice and Popular Culture, 10*(2), 109–126.

Dunn, A., & Caceres, P. J. (2010). Constructing a better estimate of police misconduct. *Policy Matters Journal,* Spring, 10–16.

References

Adams, J., Khan, H. T., Raeside, R., & White, D. I. (2007). *Research methods for graduate business and social science students*. New Delhi, India: Sage.

Albitz, R. S. (2007). The what and who of information literacy and critical thinking in higher education. *Portal: Libraries and the Academy, 7*(1), 97–109.

Alleyne, R. (2011, February 11). Welcome to the information age—174 newspapers a day. *The Telegraph*. Retrieved from http://www.telegraph.co.uk/news/science/science-news/8316534/Welcome-to-the-information-age-174-newspapers-a-day.html.

American Library Association. (2018). *Digital literacy definition*. Retrieved from http://connect.ala.org/node/181197.

American Psychological Association. (2010). *Publication manual of the American Psychological Association* (6th ed.). Washington, DC: Author.

American Psychological Association. (2018). Ethical principles of psychologists and code of conduct. *American Psychological Association Ethics Office*. Retrieved from http://www.apa.org/ethics/code/.

Andrews, D. A., Zinger, I., Hoge, R. D., Bonta, J., Gendreau, P., & Cullen, F. T. (1990). Does correctional treatment work? A clinically relevant and psychologically informed meta-analysis. *Criminology, 28*(3), 369–404.

Association of College and Research Libraries. (2000). *Information literacy competency standards for Higher education*. Retrieved from http://www.ala.org/Template.cfm?Section=Home&template=/ContentManagement/ContentDisplay.cfm&ContentID=33553.

Astolfi C. (2016). "Case dismissed, inmate released due to bad search warrant." Sandusky Register. Retrieved from http://www.sanduskyregister.com/story/201610140035.

Auriacombe, C. J. (2005). Writing research proposals for theses and dissertations in public administration: Problematic aspects of foundational skills. *Journal of Public Administration, 40*(Special issue 2), 377–391.

Babbie, E. (2001). *The practice of social research* (9th ed.). Belmont CA: Wadsworth.

Bailey, J. (2012). 5 famous plagiarists: Where are they now? *Plagiarism Today*. Retrieved from https://www.plagiarismtoday.com/2012/08/21/5-famous-plagiarists-where-are-they-now/.

Bombaro, C. (2012). *Finding history: Research methods and resources for students and scholars*. Lanham, MD: Scarecrow Press.

Breivik, P. (2005). 21st century learning and information literacy. *Change, 37*(2), 20–27.

Brewer, M., & American Library Association Office for Information Technology Policy. (2012). *Digital copyright slider*. Retrieved from http://librarycopyright.net/resources/digitalslider/index.html.

Browning, B. (2008). *Perfect phrases for writing grant proposals*. New York, NY: McGraw Hill.

Brown, L. (2014). *How to write anything: A complete guide*. New York, NY. W.W. Norton and Company.

Bui, Y. N. (2014). *How to write a master's thesis* (2nd ed.). Thousand Oaks, CA: Sage.

Business Communication. (2018). *The importance of the business letter*. Retrieved from https://thebusinesscommunication.com/importance-of-business-letter/.

CareerBuilder.com (2017). *Number of employers using social media to screen candidates at all-time high, finds latest CareerBuilder study*. Retrieved from https://www.prnewswire.com/news-releases/number-of-employers-using-social-media-to-screen-candidates-at-all-time-high-finds-latest-careerbuilder-study-300474228.html.

Cathcart, R., & Roberts, A. (2006). *Evaluating Google Scholar as a tool for information literacy*. Retrieved from https://fau.digital.flvc.org/islandora/object/fau%3A7550/datastream/OBJ/view/Evaluating_Google_Scholar_as_a_tool_for_information_literacy.pdf

Center for Innovation in Research and Teaching. (n.d.). *Overview of experimental research*. Retrieved from https://cirt.gcu.edu/research/developmentresources/research_ready/experimental/verview

Centers for Disease Control and Prevention. (n.d.). *DES research: Deciding whether a source is reliable*. Retrieved from https://www.cdc.gov/des/consumers/research/understanding_deciding.html.

CNN.com. (2003). *New York Times*: Reporter routinely faked articles. *CNN.com*. Retrieved from http://www.cnn.com/2003/US/Northeast/05/10/ny.times.reporter/.

Crossick, G. (2016). Monographs and open access. *Insights, 29*(1), 14–19.

Creswell, J. W., & Creswell, J. D. (2009). *Research design: Qualitative, quantitative, and mixed methods approaches*. Thousand Oaks, CA: Sage.

Crossick, G. (2016). Monographs and open access. *Insights, 29*(1), 14–19.

Daniel, E. (2016). The usefulness of qualitative and quantitative approaches and methods in researching problem-solving ability in science education curriculum. *Journal of Education and Practice, 7*(5), 91–100.

Davis, M. S. (1999). *Grantsmanship for criminal justice and criminology.* Thousand Oaks, CA: Sage.

Denney, A. S., & Tewksbury, R. (2013). How to write a literature review. *Journal of Criminal Justice Education, 24*(2), 218–234.

Department of Justice. (2014). *Georgia police officials and former deputy indicted by federal grand jury on charges of excessive force and obstruction of justice.* Retrieved from https://www.justice.gov/opa/pr/georgia-police-officials-and-former-deputy-indicted-federal-grand-jury-charges-excessive.

Department of Justice. (2018). Grants. Retrieved from https://www.justice.gov/grants.

Dissell, R. (2010). Words used in sexual assault police reports can help or hurt cases. *The Plains Dealer.* Retrieved from http://blog.cleveland.com/metro/2010/07/words_used_in_sexual_assault_p.html.

Doyle, A. (2018a). *How to format a business letter.* Retrieved from https://www.thebalancecareers.com/how-to-format-a-business-letter-2062540.

Doyle, A. (2018b). Tips for formatting a cover letter for a resume. *The Balance Careers.* Retrieved from https://www.thebalancecareers.com/how-to-format-a-cover-letter-2060170.

Eastern Illinois University. (2016). Scholarly monographs. Retrieved from https://booth.library.eiu.edu/subjectsPlus/subjects/guide.php?subject=monographs.

EBSCO. (2018). *Newspaper Source.* Retrieved from https://www.ebsco.com/products/research-databases/newspaper-source.

Ennis, R. (2011). The nature of critical thinking: An outline of critical thinking dispositions and abilities. Retrieved from http://faculty.education.illinois.edu/rhennis/documents/TheNatureofCriticalThinking_51711_000.pdf.

ERIC. (n.d.). *Guidance on writing abstracts.* Retrieved from https://eric.ed.gov/?abstract

Farrugia, P., Petrisor, B. A., Farrokhyar, F., & Bhandari, M. (2010). Practical tips for surgical research: Research questions, hypotheses and objectives. *Canadian Journal of Surgery (Journal canadien de chirurgie), 53*(4), 278–281.

Federal Register. (2018). Federal policy for the protection of human subjects: Delay of the revisions to the federal policy for the protection of human subjects. *Federal Register, The Daily Journal of the United States Government.* Interim Final Rule. Retrieved from https://www.federalregister.gov/documents/2018/01/22/2018-00997/federal-policy-for-the-protection-of-human-subjects-delay-of-the-revisions-to-the-federal-policy-for#_blank.

Fink, A., & Kosecoff, J. (1998). *How to conduct surveys: A step-by-step guide* (2nd ed.). Thousand Oaks, CA: Sage.

Fitzgerald, J. D., & Cox, S. M. (2002). *Research methods and statistics in criminal justice: An introduction* (3rd ed.). Belmont, CA: Wadsworth Thomson Learning.

Flaherty, M. P., & Harriston, K. A. (1994). Police credibility on trial in D.C. courts. *Washington Post.* Retrieved from http://www.washingtonpost.com/wp-srv/local/longterm/library/dc/dcpolice/94series/trainingday3.htm?noredirect=on.

Gaille, B. (2018, February 11). *25 Advantages and disadvantages of qualitative research.* Retrieved from https://brandongaille.com/25-advantages-disadvantages-qualitative-research/

Gale, P. (2014). Effective business writing: Top principles and techniques. *English Grammar.* Retrieved from https://www.englishgrammar.org/effective-business-writing/.

Gallo, A. (2014). *How to write a cover letter.* Retrieved from https://hbr.org/2014/02/how-to-write-a-cover-letter.

Garcia, A., & Lear, J. (2016, November 2). 5 stunning fake news stories that reached millions. *CNN Money.* Retrieved from http://money.cnn.com/2016/11/02/media/fake-news-stories/index.html.

Garner, B. A. (2013). *HBR guide to better business writing.* Boston, MA: Harvard Business Review Press.

Georgetown University Library. (2018). *Evaluating internet resources.* Retrieved from https://www.library.georgetown.edu/tutorials/research-guides/evaluating-internet-content.

Gerardi, D., & Wolff, N. (2008). Working together: A corrections-academic partnership that works. *Equal Opportunities International, 27*(2), 148–160.

Gilmore, J., Strickland, D., Timmerman, B., Maher, M., & Feldon, D. (2010). Weeds in the flower garden: An exploration of plagiarism in graduate students' research proposals and its connection to enculturation, ESL, and contextual factors. *International Journal for Educational Integrity, 6*(1), 13–28.

Google Scholar. (n.d.). *About*. Retrieved from https://scholar.google.com/intl/en/scholar/about.html

Grants.gov. (n.d.-a). *Grants 101*. Retrieved from https://www.grants.gov/web/grants/learn-grants/grants-101.html

Grants.gov. (n.d.-b). How to apply for grants. Retrieved from https://www.grants.gov/web/grants/applicants/apply-for-grants.html

Hacker, D. (2006). *The Bedford handbook* (7th ed.). Boston, MA: Bedford/St. Martin's.

Hancock, D. R., & Algozzine, B. (2016). *Doing case study research: A practical guide for beginning researchers*. New York, NY: Teachers College Press.

Haner, J., Wilson, K., & O'Donnell, J. (2002). Cases crumble, killers go free. *The Baltimore Sun*. Retrieved from http://www.baltimoresun.com/bal-te.murder29sep29-story.html.

Harrison, C. (2007). *Tip sheet on question wording* (Harvard University Program on Survey Research). Retrieved from https://psr.iq.harvard.edu/files/psr/files/PSRQuestionnaireTipSheet_0.pdf

Harrison, J., Weisman, D., & Zornado, J. L. (2017). *Professional writing for the criminal justice system*. New York, NY: Springer Publishing Company.

Harvey, G. (1999). *Counterargument*. Harvard, MA: Harvard College Writing Center. Retrieved from https://writingcenter.fas.harvard.edu/pages/counter-argument

Harvey, W. L. (2015). *Leadership quotes and police truisms*. Retrieved from https://www.officer.com/training-careers/article/12057342/leadership-quotes-and-police-truisms#platformComments.

Hazlett, M. (n.d.). *Suggested outline for thesis research: Comments and tips*. Unpublished manuscript.

Heitin, L. (2016). What is digital literacy? *Education Week*, 36(12), 5–6.

Heneghan, C., & Badenoch, D. (2002). *Evidence-based medicine toolkit* (2nd ed.). Oxford, England: Blackwell.

Hilbert, M., & Lopez, P. (2011). The world's technological capacity to store, communicate, and compute information. *Science*, 332(6025), 60–65. Retrieved from http://science.sciencemag.org/content/332/6025/60.

Hulley, S. B., Cummings, S. R., Browner, W. S., Grady, D. G., & Newman, T. B. (2007). *Conceiving the research question: Designing clinical research* (3rd ed.). Philadelphia, PA: Lippincott Williams & Wilkins.

Hunt, E. (2016, December 17). What is fake news? How to spot it and what you can do to stop it. *The Guardian*. Retrieved from https://www.theguardian.com/media/2016/dec/18/what-is-fake-news-pizzagate.

Jacobs, J. B. (1999). Dilemmas of corruption control. In M. A. Kleiman, F. Earls, S. Bok, & J. B. Jacobs (Eds.), *Perspective on crime and justice: 1998–1999 Lecture series* (pp. 73–93). Washington, DC: U.S. Department of Justice, National Institute of Justice.

Jick, T. D. (1979). Mixing qualitative and quantitative methods: Triangulation in action. *Administrative Science Quarterly*, 24, 602–611.

Karsh, E., & Fox, A. S. (2014). *The only grant-writing book you'll ever need*. New York, NY: Basic Books.

Kellogg, R. T. (2008). Training writing skills: A cognitive developmental perspective. *Journal of Writing Research*, 1(1), 1–26.

Kirszner, L. G., & Mandell, S. R. (2011). *Patterns for college writing: A rhetorical reader and guide* (11th ed.). Boston, MA: Bedford/St. Martin's.

Kirszner, L. G., & Mandell, S. R. (2011). *Patterns for college writing: A rhetorical reader and guide*. (12th ed.) Boston, MA: Bedford/St. Martin's.

Kong, S. C. (2014). Developing information literacy and critical thinking skills through domain knowledge learning in digital classrooms: An experience of practicing flipped classroom strategy. *Computers & Education, 78*, 160–173.

Krockow, E. M. (2018, September 27). How many decisions do we make each day? *Psychology Today*. Retrieved from https://www.psychologytoday.com/us/blog/stretching-theory/201809/how-many-decisions-do-we-make-each-day

Larson, A. (2016). What is Megan's law. Retrieved from https://www.expertlaw.com/library/criminal/megans_law.html.

Lester, J. D., & Lester, J. D., Jr. (2005). *Writing research papers: A complete guide* (11th ed.). New York, NY: Pearson Education.

Luckmann, R. (2001). Evidence-Based Medicine: How to Practice and Teach EBM, 2nd edition: By David L. Sackett, Sharon E. Straus, W. Scott Richardson, William Rosenberg, and R. Brian Haynes, Churchill Livingstone, 2000 [Book review]. *Journal of Intensive Care Medicine*, 16(3), 155–156. doi:10.1177/088506660101600307

Merriam-Webster's Dictionary. (2018). *Ethics*. Retrieved from https://www.merriam-webster.com/dictionary/ethic.

Modern Language Association. (2018). *Works cited: A quick guide. MLA Style Center, Modern Language Association.* Retrieved from https://style.mla.org/works-cited-a-quick-guide/.

National Forum on Information Literacy. (2018). National forum on information literacy 1999–2000 report. *American Library Association.* Retrieved from http://www.ala.org/aboutala/national-forum-information-literacy-1999%E2%80%932000-report.

National Institutes of Health. (2017). Rigor and reproducibility. US Department of Health and Human Services. *National Institutes of Health.* Washington, DC. Retrieved from https://grants.nih.gov/reproducibility/index.htm.

National Police Foundation. (2016). *The Kansas City preventive patrol experiment.* Retrieved from https://www.policefoundation.org/projects/the-kansas-city-preventive-patrol-experiment/

Nordquist, R. (2018). What is business writing? Definitions, tips, and examples. *ThoughtCo.* Retrieved from https://www.thoughtco.com/what-is-business-writing-1689188.

November, A. (2016). *The advanced Google searches every student should know.* Retrieved from https://november-learning.com/educational-resources-for-educators/teaching-and-learning-articles/the-advanced-google-searches-every-student-should-know/

Office of Justice Programs. (2018, November 30). *2019 OJP grant application resource guide.* Retrieved from https://ojp.gov/funding/Apply/Resources/Grant-App-Resource-Guide.htm#formatInstructions

Office of Justice Programs. (2019). *Southwest Border Rural Law Enforcement Information Sharing and Interdiction Assistance Grants: FY 2019 competitive grant solicitation.* Retrieved from https://www.bja.gov/funding/SWBI19.pdf

Paul, R. (1995). *Critical thinking: How to prepare students for a rapidly changing world.* In J. Willsen and A. Binker (Eds.). Rohnert Park, CA: Sonoma State University.

Paulas, R. (2016). On the front lines of computer literacy. *Pacific Standard. The Social Justice Foundation.* Retrieved from https://psmag.com/education/this-part-is-called-a-url.

Payne, G., & Payne, J. (2004). Objectivity. In G. Payne & J. Payne (Eds.), *Sage key concepts: Key concepts in social research* (pp. 153–157). London, England: Sage.

Phillips Jr., W. E., & Burrell, D. N. (2009). Decision-making skills that encompass a critical thinking orientation for law enforcement professionals. *International Journal of Police Science & Management, 11*(2), 141–149.

ProCon.org. (2018). *About us.* Retrieved from https://www.procon.org/about-us.php#overview

ProCon.org. (2018, May 25). *Police body cameras: Top 3 pros and cons.* Retrieved from https://www.procon.org/headline.php?headlineID=005399

Purdue OWL. (2018a). *Annotated bibliographies.* Retrieved from https://owl.english.purdue.edu/owl/owlprint/590/.

Purdue OWL. (2018b). *Parts of a memo. Purdue Online Writing Lab.* Retrieved from: https://owl.purdue.edu/owl/subject_specific_writing/professional_technical_writing/memos/parts_of_a_memo.html.

Purdue OWL. (2018c). *Resume workshop.* Retrieved from https://owl.english.purdue.edu/owl/resource/719/1/.

Purdue OWL. (2018d). *Types of APA papers.* Retrieved from https://owl.purdue.edu/owl/research_and_citation/apa_style/apa_formatting_and_style_guide/types_of_apa_papers.html

Purdue OWL (2018e). *Writing a research paper.* Retrieved from https://owl.purdue.edu/owl/general_writing/common_writing_assignments/research_papers/writing_a_research_paper.html

Purdue OWL. (n.d.). *The report abstract and executive summary.* Retrieved from https://owl.purdue.edu/owl/subject_specific_writing/writing_in_engineering/handbook_on_report_formats/abstracts_and_executive_summaries.html

Purdue University. (n.d.). Copyright infringement penalties. University Copyright Office. Purdue University. Retrieved from https://www.lib.purdue.edu/uco/—CopyrightBasics/penalties.html.

Ratcliff, C. (2018). *What are the most popular search engines?* Retrieved from https://searchenginewatch.com/2016/08/08/what-are-the-top-10-most-popular-search-engines/

Resnick, D. B. (2015). *What is ethics in research and why is it important? National Institute of Environmental Health Sciences.* Retrieved from https://www.niehs.nih.gov/research/resources/bioethics/whatis/index.cfm.

Ridley, D. (2008). *The literature review: A step-by-step guide for students.* Thousand Oaks, CA: Sage.

Rowe, S. E. (2009). Legal research, legal writing, and legal analysis: Putting law school into practice. *Stetson Law. Review, 29,* 1193.

Rugerrio, V. (2008). *Beyond feelings: A guide to critical thinking* (8th ed.). New York, NY: McGraw-Hill.

Sampson, R. J., & Raudenbush, S. W. (2004). Seeing disorder: Neighborhood stigma and the social construction of "broken windows." *Social Psychology Quarterly,* 67(4), 319–342.

Schiffhorst, G. J., & Schell, J. F. (1991). *The short handbook for writers.* New York, NY: McGraw-Hill.

Sherman, L. W., Schmidt, J. D., Rogan, D. P., & Smith, D. A. (1992). The variable effects of arrest on criminal careers: The Milwaukee domestic violence experiment. *Journal of Criminal Law & Criminology,* 83, 137–169.

Shultz, M. (2007). Comparing test searches in PubMed and Google Scholar. *Journal of the Medical Library Association: JMLA,* 95(4), 442–445.

Smith, D. (2003). Five principles for research ethics. *Monitor on Psychology, 34*(1), 56. Retrieved from http://www.apa.org/monitor/jan03/principles.aspx.

Stake, R. E. (1995). *The art of case study research.* Thousand Oaks, CA: Sage.

Stanford's Key to Information Literacy. (2018). What is information literacy? Retrieved from http://skil.stanford.edu/intro/research.html.

Sutton, J., & Austin, Z. (2015). Qualitative research: Data collection, analysis, and management. *Canadian Journal of Hospital Pharmacy,* 68(3), 226–231. doi:10.4212/cjhp.v68i3.1456

Technopedia.com. (2018). *Computer literate.* Retrieved from https://www.techopedia.com/definition/23303/computer-literate.

Theobald, M. A. (n.d.). *Statistics and data analysis.* Unpublished manuscript.

Thistlethwaite, A. B., & Wooldredge, J. (2010). *Forty studies that changed criminal justice.* Upper Saddle River, NJ: Prentice Hall.

University of North Carolina at Chapel Hill. (2019). *Literature reviews.* Retrieved from https://writingcenter.unc.edu/tips-and-tools/literature-reviews/

University of Southern California Libraries. (2019). *Organizing your social sciences research paper: 3. The abstract.* Retrieved from https://libguides.usc.edu/writingguide/abstract

University of Southern Indiana. (2019). *Common components of land proposals.* Retrieved from https://www.usi.edu/ospra/grant-proposal-and-federal-contract-development/common-components-of-grant-proposals/

University of Washington–Tacoma. (2018). Criminal justice: Source types: Peer-reviewed & scholarly & more. Retrieved from http://guides.lib.uw.edu/c.php?g=344206&p=2319662.

U.S. Copyright Office. (n.d.). *Copyright in general.* Retrieved from https://www.copyright.gov/help/faq/faq-general.html#what

VandenBos, G. R. (2010). Foreword. In *Publication manual of the American Psychological Association* (6th ed.). Washington, DC: American Psychological Association.

Vollmer, A. (1936). *The police and modern society: Plain talk based on practical experience.* Berkeley: University of California Press.

Ward, D. (2006). Revisioning information literacy for lifelong meaning. *The Journal of Academic Librarianship,* 32, 396–402.

Weiler, A. (2005). Information-seeking behavior in generation Y students: Motivation, critical thinking, and learning theory. *The Journal of Academic Librarianship,* 31, 46–53.

Wertz, R.E.H., Fosmire, M., Purzer, S. Saragih, A. I., Van Epps, A. S., Sapp Nelson, M. R., & Dillman, B. G. (2013). Work in progress: Critical thinking and information literacy: Assessing student performance. Unpublished manuscript presented at the 12th annual American Society for Engineering Education Conference. Presented at the 120th ASEE Annual Conference & Exposition, Atlanta, GA, American Society for Engineering Education.

Wikipedia: About. (2018). *Wikipedia.org.* https://en.wikipedia.org/wiki/Wikipedia:About.

Wilson, C., & Brewer, N. (1992). One-and two-person patrols: A review. *Journal of Criminal Justice,* 20(5), 443–454.

Wisdom, J., & Creswell, J. W. (2013). *Mixed methods: Integrating quantitative and qualitative data collection and analysis while studying patient-centered medical home models* (AHRQ Publication No. 13-0028-EF). Rockville, MD: Agency for Healthcare Research and Quality.

Wonacott, M. E. (2001). *Technological literacy. ERIC Digest.* Retrieved from https://www.ericdigests.org/2002-3/literacy.htm. Eric Identifier ED459371.

Writing Center of Wisconsin–Madison. (2018). *Writing cover letters.* Retrieved from https://writing.wisc.edu/Handbook/CoverLetters.html.

Yin, R. K. (2009). *Case study research: Design and methods* (4th ed.). Thousand Oaks, CA: Sage.

Yin, R. K. (2012). *Applications of case study research* (3rd ed.). Thousand Oaks, CA: Sage.

Yin, R. K. (2014). *Case study research design and methods* (5th ed.). Thousand Oaks, CA: Sage.